CELEBRATING THE YORKSHIRE DALES

MIKE APPLETON

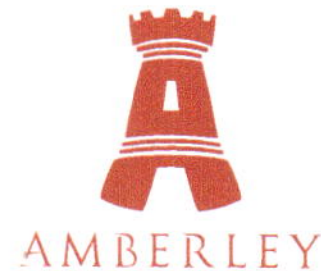

AMBERLEY

First published 2026

Amberley Publishing, The Hill, Stroud
Gloucestershire GL5 4EP

www.amberley-books.com

British Library Cataloguing in Publication Data.
A catalogue record for this book is available from the British Library.

ISBN 978 1 3981 2274 1 (print)
ISBN 978 1 3981 2275 8 (ebook)

Typeset by Simon and Sons ITES Services Pvt. Ltd., Chennai, India.
Printed in Great Britain.

Appointed GPSR EU Representative:
Easy Access System Europe Oü, 16879218
Address: Mustamäe tee 50, 10621, Tallinn, Estonia
Contact Details: gpsr.requests@easproject.com, +358 40 500 3575

Contents

Introduction

I was listening to an interview with British journalist and writer Anita Sethi about her book *I Belong Here: A Journey Along the Backbone of Britain* (2021) when she spoke about much of the northern countryside being a wounded landscape. Words such as scar, force, gorge and crag demonstrate the fabric of our National Parks being torn and worked by geological forces, with people on the land working within their constraints.

At the same time, almost serendipitously, I was approached by Nick Grant at Amberley Publishing to pen a celebration of my favourite National Park – the Yorkshire Dales. I'd written five other homages to this special place and was unsure whether a sixth lay within. Anita fixed that. Her words evoked an emotional response as to why I love this landscape; I am 'hefted' to it, and I want to continue to show people that it's not just sheep and rolling fells.

I then asked a friend about what they liked about this place. They said: 'A combination: the fabulous landscape and its wildlife, the local communities and their support for where they live. There is always something going on, great places to walk and eat, and the dramatic weather. I could go on, but I'll probably bore the pants off you…' How could I not respond?

The chapters in this book celebrate some of my favourite things about the Yorkshire Dales. I could have waxed lyrical for thousands of words, but each passage returns to a similar theme. It's the people of the Dales who make it special, and I celebrate every one of them.

In no particular order, I'd like to thank Nick Grant and the team at Amberley Publishing; archaeologist and historian Dr David Johnson; my favourite Dales authors Susan Parry, Diane Allen and Julia Chapman; Tanya Carter at Limestone Books in Settle; Pat Halliwell and John Webb at Craven Pothole Club; Brian Varley and his daughter Louise; my confidant and caving friend John Cordingley; Bill Nix and his amazing cave photography; Andrew and Sally Hattan at Low Riggs Farm; Sarah Binks-Lambert and Fiona Rosher at Dales Countryside Museum; Knitting experts Angharad Thomas, Kathleen Kinder and Penny Hemmingway; Leigh Weston and Neil Heseltine at Hill Top Farm; Emmeline Butler, Elizabeth Sullivan and Patrick Wardle at the National Trust; Susan Briggs from Dales Discoveries;

Andrew Fagg and Adrian Shepherd from the Yorkshire Dales National Park Authority; David Joy MBE; Mollie Hanson and Stephen Dennis at Bentham Auction Mart; Zanna Dennis from the Livestock Auctioneers Association; Roger Ingham MBE and Victoria Benn; Mike Harding, Bob Pegg, Richard Hargreaves, Rachel and Mike Benson, Mark Wallace and the late Bob Ellis for their traditional Dales musical expertise; David Felton and Mark Richards at the Countrystride podcast for their interview with Angus Winchester, Professor Emeritus of Local & Landscape History at Lancaster University; Sarah Fleetwood from the Farmer Network; John and Judith Dawson at Bleak Bank Farm; Janet Rawlins and her *A Dales Countryside Cookbook*; Marie Hartley and Joan Ingilby; Hannah Rose; and my colleagues at Yorkshire Dales Millennium Trust.

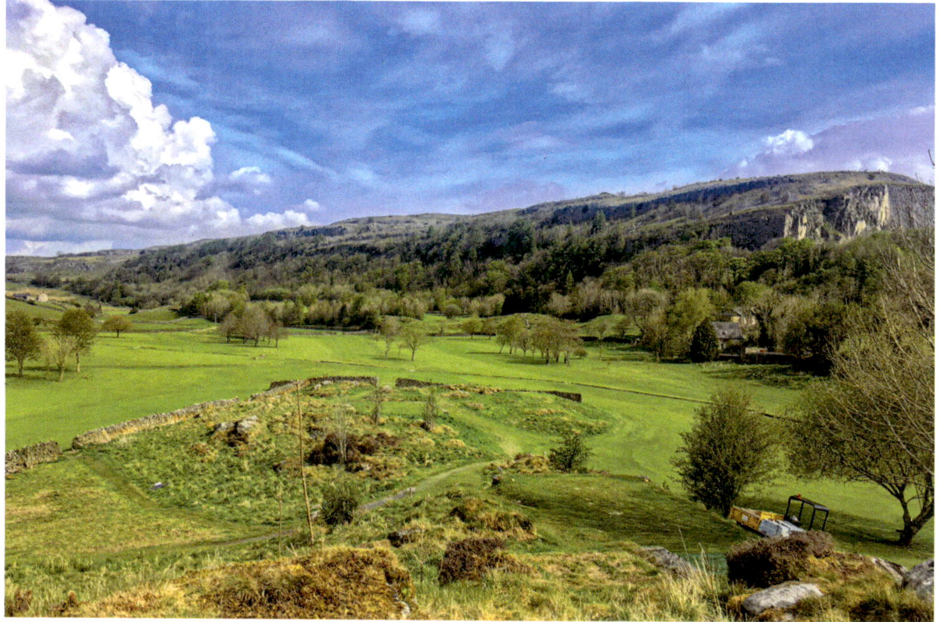

The impressive Giggleswick Scar.

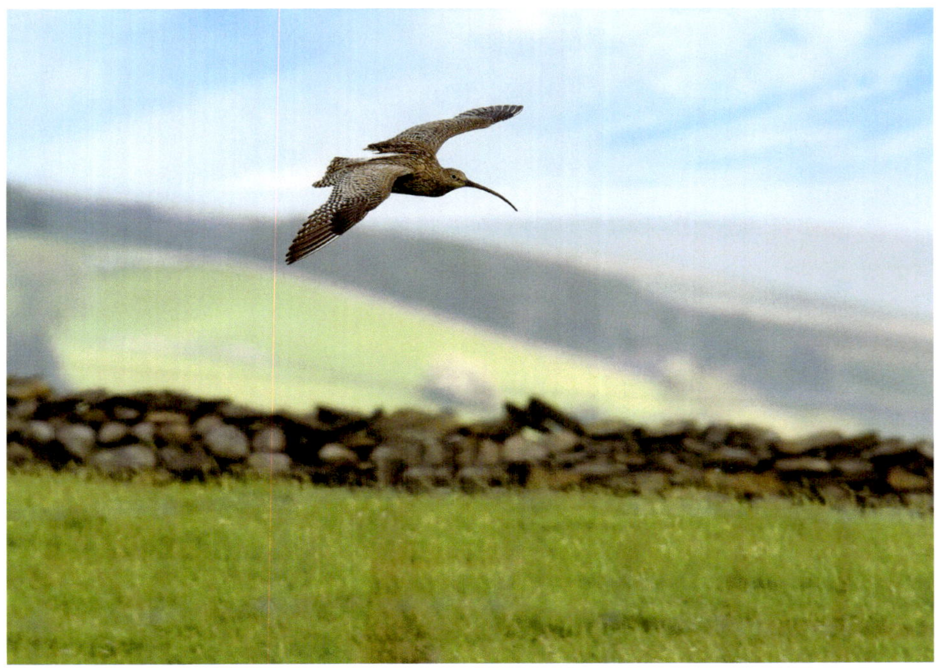

Curlew at Helwith Bridge. (Mik Cardus)

Auction Marts

The image of the lonely farmer crossing the tops with their flock has been eulogised in several paintings. Artists have pondered over the majestic scene; sheepdogs keeping their charges in line whilst their owner leans towards the wind, hail and whatever the Dales weather has to throw at them. These hardy folk took their sheep to market on drovers' roads, tracks that crisscrossed the countryside, often following routes scratched in the earth long before them. Near Ingleton, for example, they would have walked in the footsteps of Romans along a road that supplied the Virosidum fort just north of near Bainbridge.

Then at the instantly recognisable Ribblehead, pre and post its construction in 1876, there would have been a cacophony of noise as man met man, sheep met sheep, and sales, catch-ups and fun took place. These somewhat informal markets, in the modern sense, were the mainstay of trade and maintained not only an income for those who worked the land but a sense of community too. Makeshift markets occurred in villages across the National Park – The Dales Countryside Museum in Hawes has two wonderful pictures of people gathered for a sheep fair in Leyburn marketplace in 1906 and a sheep sale outside the Listers in Malham four years later.

The community of these meeting places still linger at shows and festivals throughout the year. More 'official' markets in the Park now exist in Hawes, Skipton, in the far north at Kirkby Stephen, at J36 of the M6, and Bentham.

Auction marts do a staggering amount of trade and work to help keep farming viable. According to the Livestock Auctioneers' Association, in 2023, 3,962,000 store and breeding livestock went through markets in England and Wales. When you add 'finished' livestock of 6,993,000, including cattle, pigs and sheep, the figure rises to 10,955,000. This brings in a total turnover of £2,224,634,000 – not insignificant by any means to the livelihoods of the countryside.

Established in 1903, Bentham Auction Mart is still linked to Richard Turner and Son Auctioneers, founded some 100 years earlier by Bentham farmer Robert Turner. At the beginning of the twentieth century, many farmers in the area were tenants who didn't have a secure tenure on their land. This meant they often sought better rent elsewhere, moving their livestock, or selling them on. These dispersal sales would take place at fairs, local pubs, or on the farm, under the auspices of a knowledgeable and fair auctioneer. In Bentham's case, this was undertaken by the Turners.

As this 'business' progressed, Richard Turner met with William Mitchell of Lancaster, who owned the Royal Oak Hotel in the village, and formed a plan to create a more official auction mart. William proposed building a suitable space, which he would lease to a Company formed and duly registered to operate an auction mart. All he asked for was 3 per cent per year on his investment – which worked out at around £20 a year – and the new company had to operate the site for ten years. He was canny, as the mart was on the doorstep of his hotel. Richard also wanted to bring people together under one roof to ensure transparency.

Some 165 people arrived to hear about Richard and William's proposal, and the minutes showed that 'A show of hands was taken, after some discussion, and an overwhelming majority decided to form a Company.' The new mart was to have provision to accommodate 200 sheep and 30 head of cattle and was built by local contractor Henry Slinger.

Stephen Dennis is the current Senior Auctioneer and Market Manager at Bentham and says that the original ethos of serving the local community is still very much part of what drives the business.

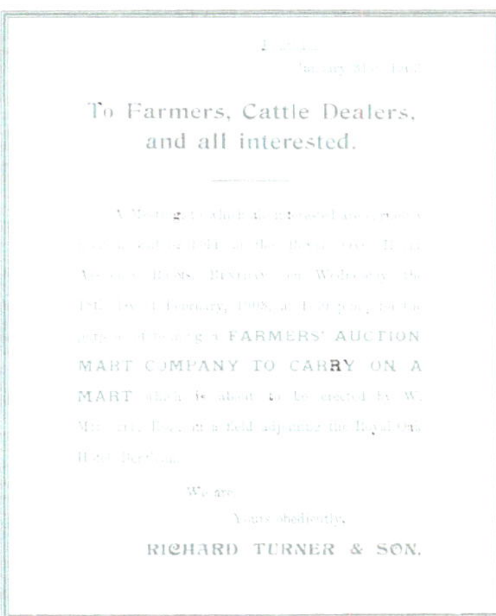

To Farmers, Cattle Dealers,
and all interested.

FARMERS' AUCTION MART COMPANY TO CARRY ON A MART which is about to be erected by W. Mitchell, Esq., in a field adjoining the Royal Oak Hotel, Bentham.

We are,
Yours obediently,
RICHARD TURNER & SON.

This handbill was distributed locally to raise interest in the possible establishment of an Auction Mart in Bentham.

The original notice to gauge interest in an auction mart. (Bentham Auction Mart)

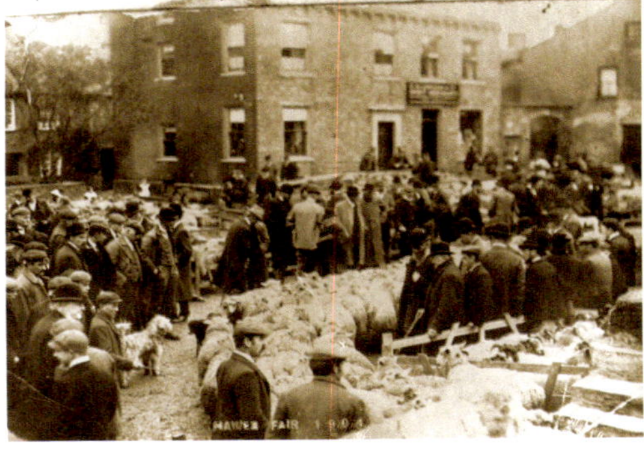

A sheep fair at the marketplace in Hawes. Sheep are gathered in wooden pens on both sides of the road – imagine the noise! (Dales Countryside Museum, Yorkshire Dales National Park Authority)

'Although we have expanded somewhat, we have remained on the site for the last 120 years,' he said. 'We are still very much part of the community and welcome most of the time, even though we may cause a few traffic jams now and again.

'Marts like ours are vital as they offer transparency and create an environment for healthy competition. Every purchaser is treated with the same terms whether you are a supermarket or a butcher wishing to buy a small number of stock. Here, farmers aren't at the mercy of someone buying directly from the farm without the benefit of competition. We set a fair price in a transparent trading platform and a range of customers ensure people get a fair, competitive price. We pay promptly too, which is a real benefit for farmers as it means they aren't chasing bad debt.

'Then you have the community point of view. We bring farmers together and they share their problems. Not every farmer who comes to us will be buying or selling; it is a great place for them to meet and realise they're not on their own and the problems they're experiencing are often experienced by others. This is a vital and often overlooked service we provide.'

The Livestock Auctioneers Association's (LAA) *More than a Mart: The Role of UK Livestock Auction Markets in Rural Communities* (2021) highlighted how important the auction mart is beyond the sale:

Markets were seen as, potentially, a critically important antidote to this social isolation for those still able and willing to attend. Few respondents reported socialising outside of market day, and for those who stated that they frequently socialised off-farm, they knew of many more who were unlikely to leave the farm

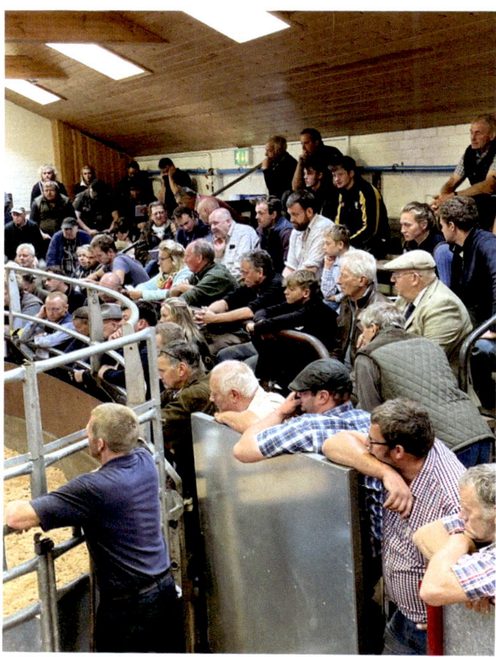

Farmers watching sales at Bentham Auction Mart. (Bentham Auction Mart)

specifically to socialise, unless it involved attending the market. Moreover, some agricultural discussion groups and farmer networking groups use the mart location to meet, further emphasising the role of the mart outside of the sales arena. Some of our farmer respondents, of varying ages and farm types and sizes, attended the mart even if not buying or selling. Auction managers estimated that between 5% and 20% of mart attendees tended to come for social reasons only. Many of these are older or retired farmers for whom the mart was important as a hub for social opportunities. At many markets, it was clear that the mart community tended to 'keep an eye' on how the older attendees were and if they were present on any given day. It seemed that the café and the ability to get a hot meal was also high on their priorities, and some retired farmers would travel to several markets a week throughout the region simply to meet with peers and enjoy the mart experience.

The team at Bentham take this 'unofficial' welfare role seriously, particularly when busy, and they know most of their customers well. It is a family relationship and was vital during the 2020 Covid-19 pandemic. Social isolation was an issue for most, yet it hit hardest in rural areas. Farmers were able to watch sales through the internet and have some semblance of normality, but it wasn't the same as the hustle of a busy sale and meeting your friends face to face. Marts across the country provide a vital service and there are several that house health hubs with nurses and other important support facilities. As the LAA report says, these venues are more than just a mart.

'Our main thrust is the marketing of sheep and cattle,' Stephen continues. 'We are likely to be within the country's three or four top sheep markets and quite often we will sell the highest volume of sheep of any of the markets throughout England. That has grown over the last twenty years and is largely down to the team of staff that we have here.

'A lot of it is down old-fashioned networking, communicating within the farming community on a one-to-one level and keeping in contact with our customers. We give them personal feedback and advice, and this is important following the pandemic. Some of our sales will see a large attendance depending on what is being sold, but we have noticed that some farmers aren't staying around to see their stock sold; the pandemic meant we livestreamed our sales, and some now prefer to stay at home and watch their sale there. It's a shame but understandable as times have changed.'

Change is not just confined to the pandemic. Rural areas are undergoing some of the biggest transformative changes in land use since the Second World War. Farmers will lose their basic payments by 2027, and although there will be Environmental Land Management schemes, they won't cover the income lost under subsidy. This will be felt hardest in the uplands.

In 2024, lamb prices were good, helping to soften the blow, but prices do fluctuate. Stephen says: 'The level of bureaucracy for farmers is challenging. I think the message coming from the government and society to some degree is that farmers are being undervalued and told they're not required. There's an extremely slow push towards the environment and the message to farmers is 'we will pay you not to farm'.

We'll pay you to produce less. That is having a demoralising effect on the farming community, and we're effectively telling them that what they're good at is no longer valued. Governments and society seem happy to import cheap food from abroad, rather than grow it at home. Sadly, I think that's something that will come home to roost, and the health and welfare of the farming community will suffer.

'We're already seeing flock and herd reductions, and in some cases, dispersals. Some of that is related to the age of farmers and the lack of succession. It is no longer viable for a medium-sized family farm, which was once a viable unit, to continue. People can't maintain a living from those small family farms, so you see them sold off for residential and other uses.'

'Then you have flock reductions due to changing farming practices such as environmental schemes, low-input systems and such.'

He continued: 'It is somewhat demoralising. There will be less stock available to sell, which will of course affect us, but what is more troublesome is the fact they are wasting generations of work that our forebears have sought to produce and bring the land into the productive state it is now. You can waste in five years what it takes 300 years to develop.'

It's a stark thought but one that is on the lips of many farmers across the Dales. The next few years are likely to define agriculture for the next century. In the meantime, Bentham Auction Mart, like others in the Park, will continue to champion farmers and look after their wellbeing. You can find out more and visit the mart here: www.benthamauction.co.uk

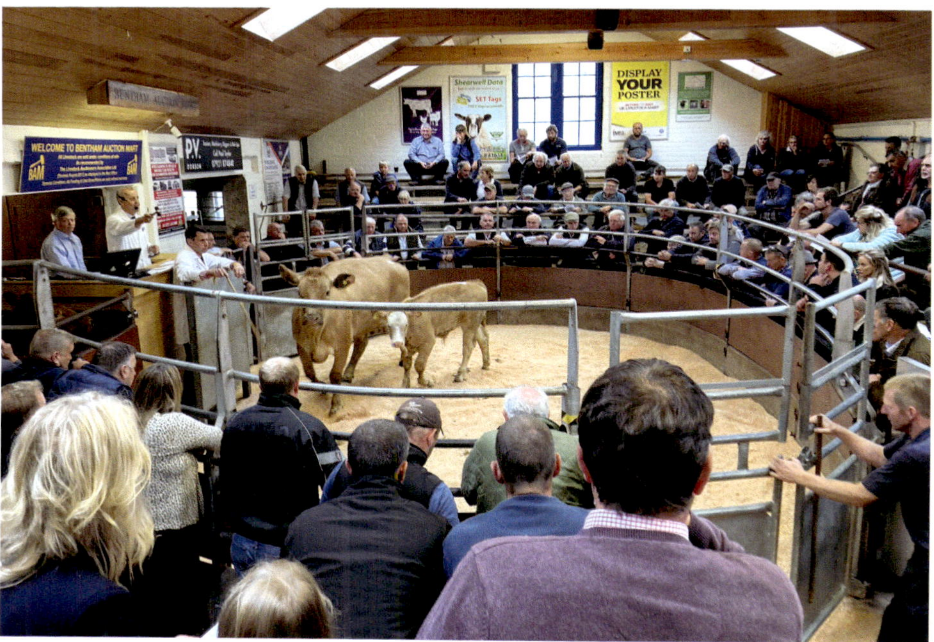

Cattle for sale. (Bentham Auction Mart)

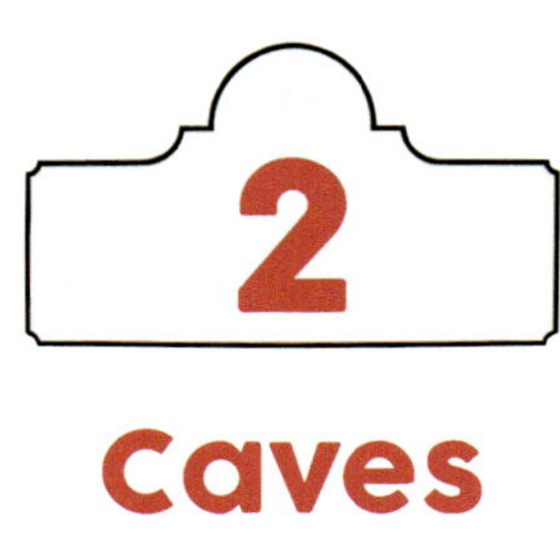

Caves

There probably isn't a more iconic pothole in the world than Gaping Gill. Impressive above and below ground, Fell Beck meanders along the hillside until it plunges 322 feet (98 metres) into an open chasm. The pothole was first bottomed in 1895 after several previous attempts inched closer to its floor. John Birkbeck reached a ledge at around 58 metres in 1842 – and this bears his name today. But it was the much-travelled and revered French caver Édouard-Alfred Martel, the father of speleology, who finally hit the bottom in 1895 by rope ladder. Subsequent explorations have found more than 15 kilometres of passage and a link – now blocked – to Ingleborough Cave down the valley.

There are several ways into the system, but all are out of bounds to non-cavers apart from the showcave at Ingleborough Cave. Those having a look around the large surface entrance to Gaping Gill could easily find their way to the bottom via one slip at the various holes near the shaft. In flood, it is an awe-inspiring and positively frightful sight. One side route in particular – the Rat Hole – looks innocuous, but after a crawl, concealed holes in the floor, if missed, could see you head right to the bottom. Around the Gill are other entrances, including Disappointment Pot, Flood Entrance, Stream Passage Pot, and the more obvious Bar Pot, which is just over the stile as you head towards Gaping Gill from Trow Gill.

For those who aren't experienced cavers, there is an opportunity to be winched down the shaft courtesy of the volunteers of Craven Pothole Club and Bradford Pothole Club. These meets occur around the spring bank holiday and in mid-August. To be inside Gaping Gill and looking up at the small waterfall coming from the surface is something else. There's a charge, of course, and the standing joke is that you're only charged for the ascent back out. Very kind of them.

The first winch was by the Yorkshire Ramblers Club in 1896. They had tried to follow Martel's lead in using rope ladders but couldn't make it. Not to be beaten, they opted to use a bosun's chair lowered by rope from a simple hand-operated windlass.

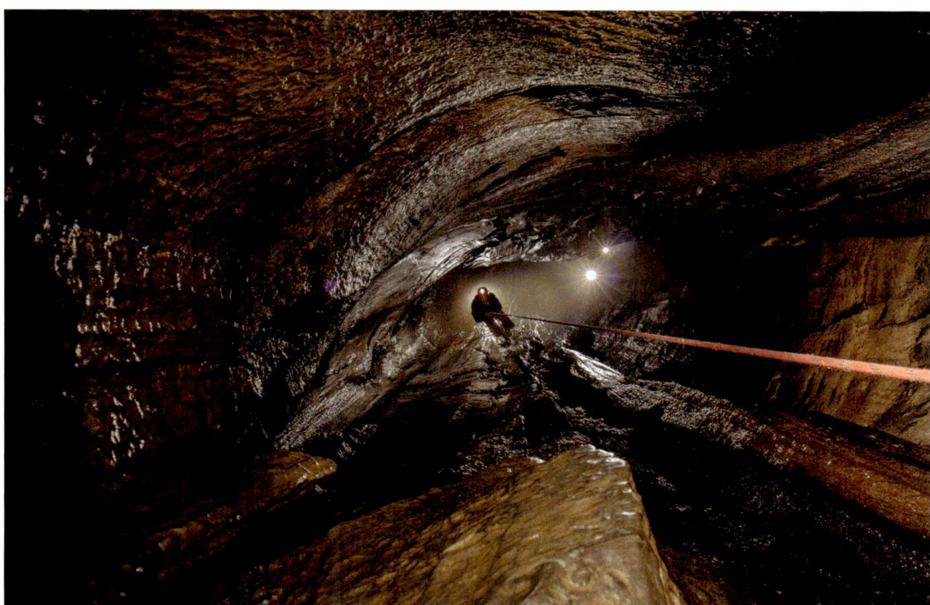

Craven Pothole Club (CPC) member John Cordingley writes:

This would be hung from a wooden jib in a small side tunnel next to the Main Shaft, allowing a direct descent of the alternative 'Lateral Shaft'. On 9 May 1896, descending via what is still known as 'Jib Tunnel', they made it to the bottom on what was effectively the first true Gaping Gill winch meet.

CPC's first official winch meet was in 1932, a year after they completed a descent of the Main Shaft on wood and rope ladders. The club borrowed a wooden gantry belonging to the Yorkshire Ramblers Club and constructed a simple hand windlass. The early Yorkshire Speleological Association also held winches around the turn of last century and the British Speleological Association hosted one after the Second World War in 1946.

CPC member John Webb is part of the crew that sets up the winch before the mid-August meet. He says it is an intense time in the build-up, especially as the many tents and equipment are put in place, but it is a real cavers' village with people coming together to celebrate one of the Dales' natural wonders.

'I joined the CPC in 1973,' he said. 'I remember going down the shaft for the first time, and I was very apprehensive. In those days, the winch was operated by a gravity/brake system and not by hydraulic power as it is now. It was cold too and I remember thinking I hope the driver knows what he is doing. Thankfully,

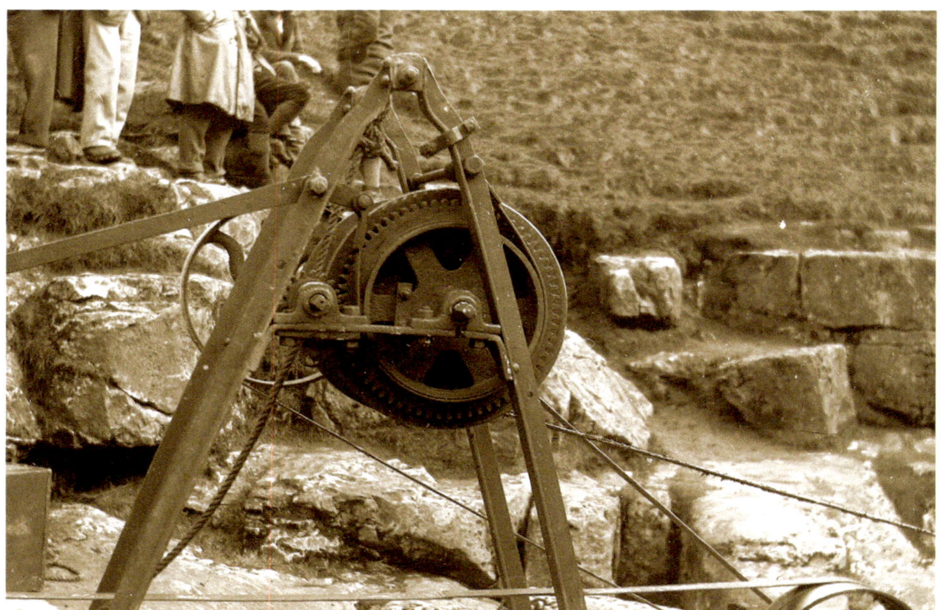

A close-up of the original Yorkshire Ramblers Club winch that was used in the 1930s. (The Craven Pothole Club archive)

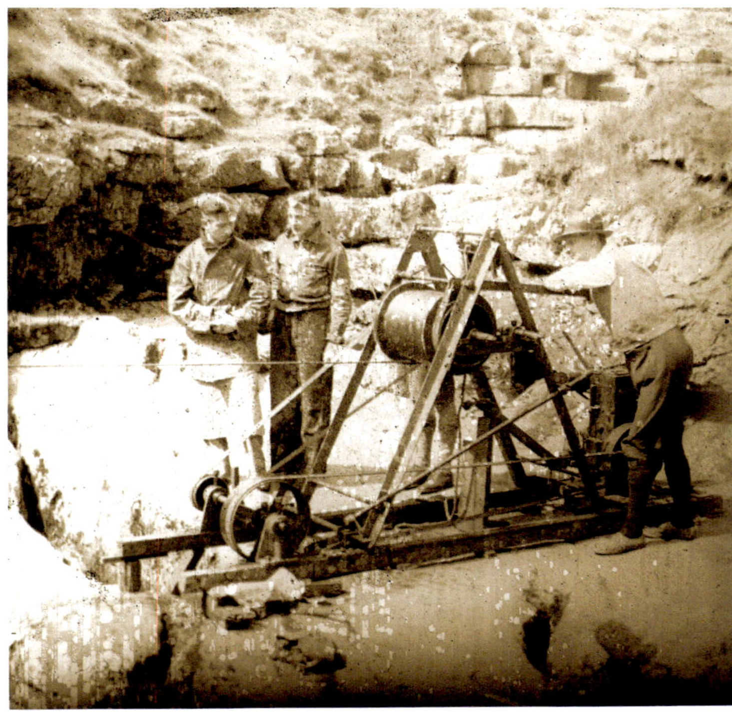

Jim Hill in charge of the winch in 1938. (The Craven Pothole Club archive)

he let me down slowly, which was magnificent as I could see everything on the way down. I saw Birkbeck's Ledge, where the water came in, and the surface entrance getting smaller as I descended. When you compare that to a year later when I was helping to set it up … well, they just fired me down as quickly as possible.

'The meet was a real eye-opener. In those early days, I would live up there for two weeks in a tent and we would have a really good time. I remember that the refreshment tent back then was quite close to the entrance shaft and care was needed when exiting for your "home" tent. Then, there were storms and floods. I remember in the eighties and early nineties when the odd hurricane came through and demolished the mess tent.'

John currently looks after some of the tent logistics whilst the rest of the club's volunteers set up the winch and all the other associated equipment and facilities. He says the meet has certainly changed over the years, especially with people queuing for hours to enjoy the experience. The winch meet has become very popular for those wanting to tick off an adventure and has been publicised on TV and social media.

He continued: 'The winch itself has changed to a hydraulic system. It means the ride is smooth and probably around ninety seconds each way. Before, it was about a minute's "freefall" braked descent under gravity, with a mechanical engine belt drive for the return, just in the same way as a bicycle chain works. And then there is the social side. The fact that we have now got a 5-metre square

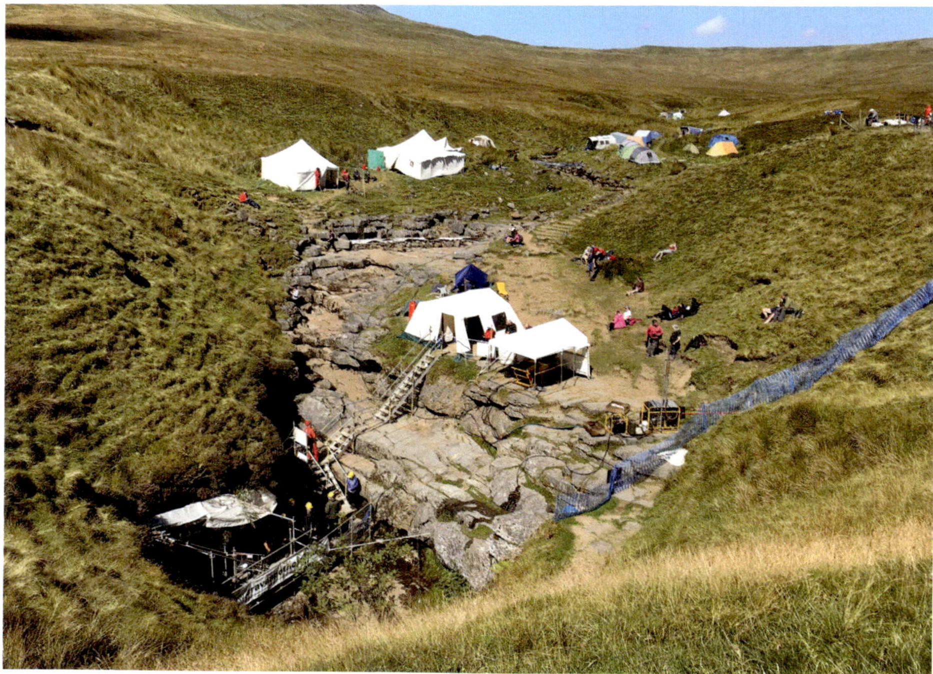

A more modern view of the gantry. (John Cordingley)

marquee for relaxing after winching shows how far the meet has progressed. People will transport their gear, but we also use farmers who will take trailer loads of equipment up to the site for us. It's a far cry from the simple operation it used to be. Each year, you will learn something new and take the improvement forward to the next.'

Sending people down a 322-foot pitch on a chair is an important job when it comes to health and safety. The set-up is regimentally planned, and the safety of the public is vital.

'I think the gantry/trapdoor probably has the biggest associated risk because if the operator got it wrong, heaven forbid, it's a fair way down to the bottom,' John added: 'The winch-driver's role is very important too and we have procedures in place to ensure that we don't allow anybody to do jobs until they've been trained, mentored, and observed by somebody else who has had experience in the role before. We cover the risks and there are a lot of fail-safes in the system.'

John estimates that since 1932, CPC has lowered almost 100,000 people into the Main Hall and believes it is only going to get more popular.

'I've been in the booking-in tent early in the morning, well before 8 a.m., looked out and been astounded at the queue going up and around the shakehole. We've had people from London turning up after a six-hour drive and a steady line of people walking up from Clapham in the wee hours. On one meet, I closed the bookings at

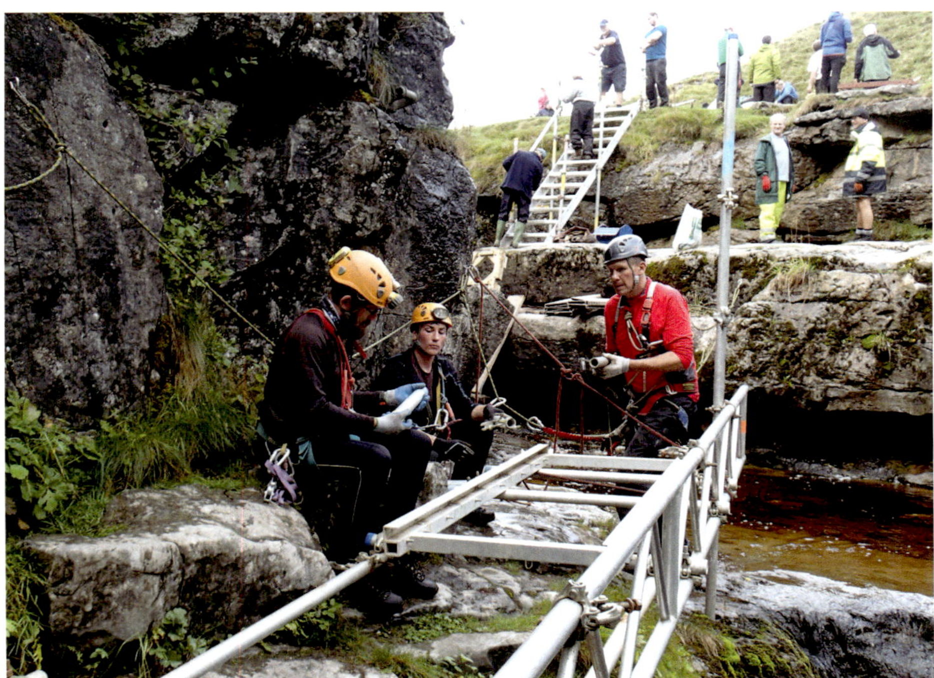

Building the gantry … (John Cordingley)

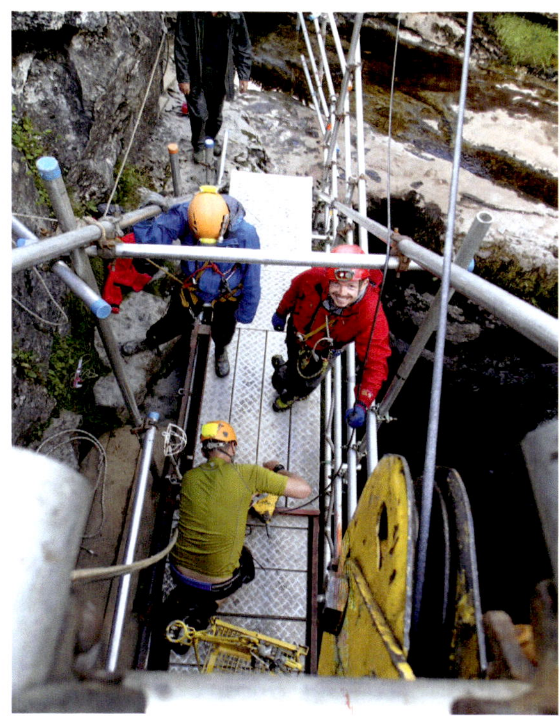

Right and below: … is a time-consuming job. (John Cordingley)

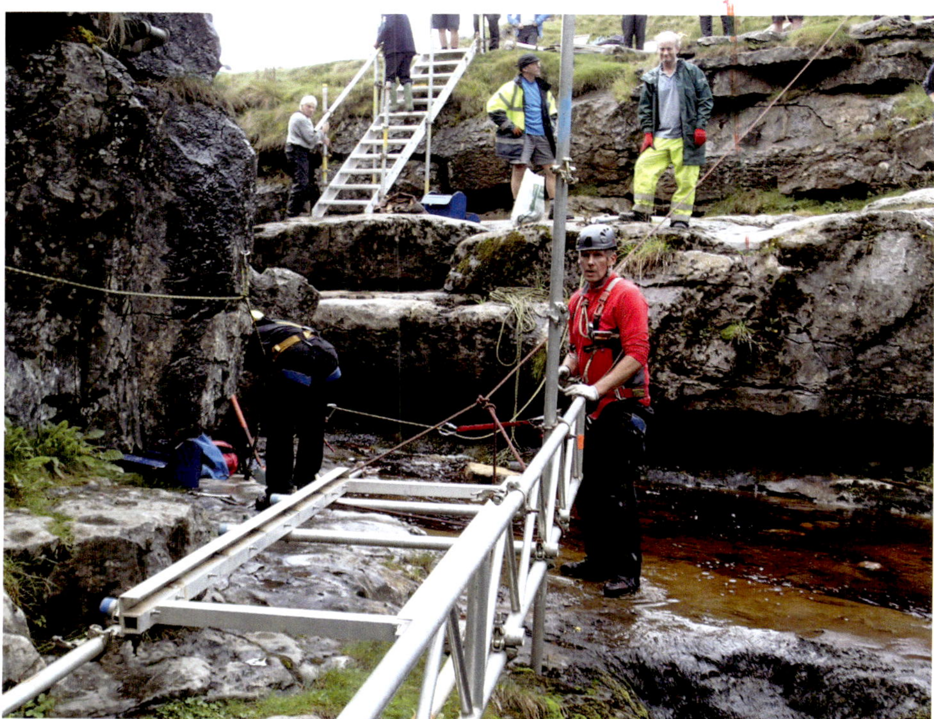

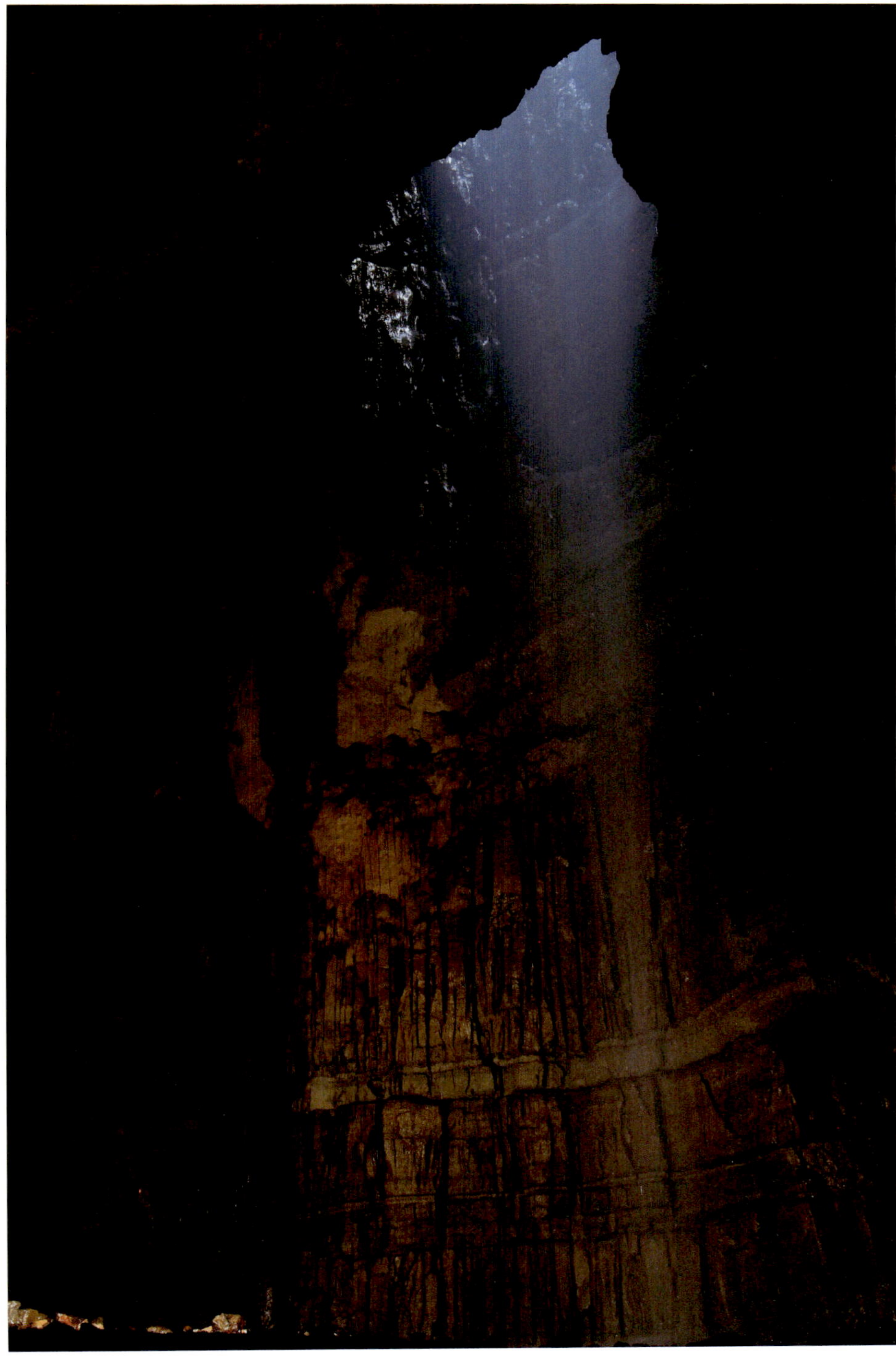

The magnificent Main Shaft of Gaping Gill. (Bill Nix)

10.45 a.m. because it was that busy. I wouldn't let that put people off though; it is an amazing place to visit, you just need to plan ahead and book in advance.'

Brian Varley joined Craven Pothole Club in 1950, although he happily says he avoided paying his dues until 1952, and has the distinction of being the person who discovered the longest stalactite in the British Isles at Poll an Ionain, now known as Doolin Cave, in County Clare. He was part of the early winch meets and says the set-up was very different from now.

'It was wooden, and I suppose it looked like gallows,' he explained. 'It had two main beams that went across the shaft and another that was secured onto a stone ledge, which was maybe 13 inches down the pitch. Then, it had a square frame with a wheel on the top and a rope heading to the chair. After a while, we decided to use a four-stroke Pettis engine, which I altered to make sure it would work efficiently. The original bosun chair had a piece of wood for the seat and a wrought-iron frame. It had a big, thick black leather belt with two hooks on it. The rope from the wheel was fixed around the eye of the chair and then came down and clicked into your belt. For access to the pitch, a plank was removed, and down you went. There was one cable in those days, but for insurance purposes, we soon moved to two. We changed to aluminium supports from wood in around 1960.'

Brian is CPC's oldest and now longest-serving member, and whilst he doesn't cave anymore – and who can blame him at over ninety years old – he tries and attends club dinners. That said, he did return to Sleets Gill in Lower Littondale at the age of eighty-eight. He says one of the best things about the meet was the camaraderie, which was strong and perhaps a little wild at times.

'Some of the people up there would have slug-balancing competitions,' he added. 'They'd gather big black slugs from all over the fell and then have a competition to see who could get the most slugs on their head. I guess that was tame, looking back. We'd also walk down to Clapham for a few beers and then walk back up. I honestly don't know how we didn't fall down a big hole because we were staggering around the place that much. That was a long time ago, though.'

Gaping Gill is thought to be around 30 metres deeper than the official depth because of the amount of fill on the floor. That would make the pitch some 130 metres (427 feet) deep. If only people could be persuaded to bring out a rock or two on their visit…

The Dales has several long pitches that are classics among cavers. Long Kin West on the slopes of Ingleborough has shafts of 91 metres (299 feet) and 55 metres (180 feet). Across the fell is Nick Pot, a small, tight-looking entrance that hides its secrets. Inside is Vulcan Pot with a 101-metre pitch (331 feet), although the route is now described as 'unstable due to lots of fault breccia, and consequently is not fitted with resin anchors and is therefore not recommended' by the Council for the Northern Caving Community. They describe the cave as having four entrances, with Thornber's Entrance joining Vulcan Pot on a shelf called Traverse in the Gods around 30 metres down.

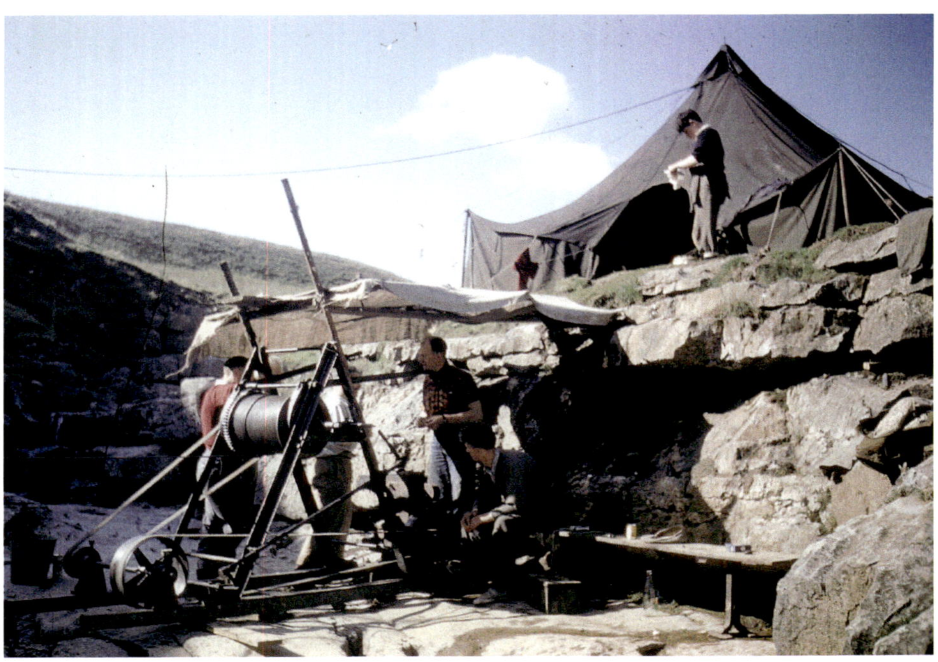

Brian Varley (in the red-checked shirt) with Len Cook at the CPC winch meet in 1960. (The Craven Pothole Club archive)

The Dales doesn't have its own way, though, as on New Year's Day in 1999, an even deeper shaft was discovered in the nearby Peak District – Titan – at 142 metres (466 feet) deep!

You can find out more about the Craven Pothole Club at www. cravenpotholeclub.org

Film

It's easy to see why the Yorkshire Dales would be popular with TV and movie makers. As a child, I remember watching the telly and seeing a helicopter sweeping over Malham Cove for Barrett Homes, while I'm sure those of a certain vintage will recall Ted Moult's 'Fit the best, Everest' ads being filmed at the Tan Hill Inn above Reeth.

Gordale Scar, just around the corner from Malham Cove, featured as the secret valley of the 'Mystics' in *The Dark Crystal* (1982), the first fully-animatronic feature film, directed by Muppet creators Jim Henson and Frank Oz.

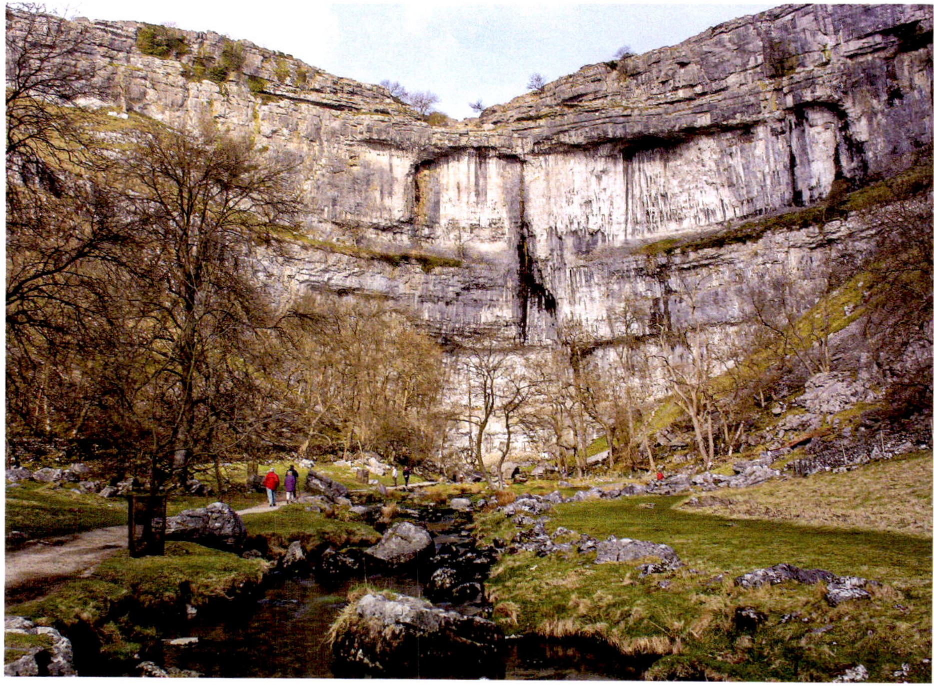

Malham Cove is well-known and dramatic on film.

Andrew Fagg from the National Park Authority tells me that season two of Netflix's fantasy series *The Witcher* (2019) features the Scar and nearby Janet's Foss. The Cove made an appearance in *Harry Potter and the Deathly Hallows: Part 1* (2010) and the 1992 version of *Wuthering Heights*, whilst in 1951, Bette Davis' *Another Man's Poison* featured Malham village and Malham Tarn. The limestone pavement at the top of the Cove is part of *Slipstream* (1989) as Bob Peck is chased by a microlight. *Calendar Girls* (2003) was filmed in Kettlewell, Settle, Skipton, Burnsall and Kilnsey.

Elsewhere, Hardraw Force and Aysgarth saw regular visits from the cast and crew of *Robin Hood: Prince of Thieves* (1991), one of my favourite films. Robin of the Hood, as Marian describes him, and played by Kevin Costner, bathes in the waters underneath the 100-foot waterfall after daubing himself in manure to get into a castle. Ironically, it wasn't Costner's backside on camera in the plunge pool but rather a body double, and a no doubt cold one at that. At the upper Aysgarth Falls, Costner meets what would later become Robin's merry men and takes an unfortunate dip after being tripped up during a heist.

On TV, the starring role of the Dales also comes to the fore. Channel 5's *Anne Boleyn* (2020) was shot at Bolton Castle, a historic venue well worth visiting, while *All Creatures Great and Small* is home to scenes from Askrigg, Swaledale, Arkengarthdale and Langthwaite as well as, more recently, Grassington. Documentaries are aplenty too with Amanda Owen's *Our Yorkshire Farm* shot at her house in Ravenseat.

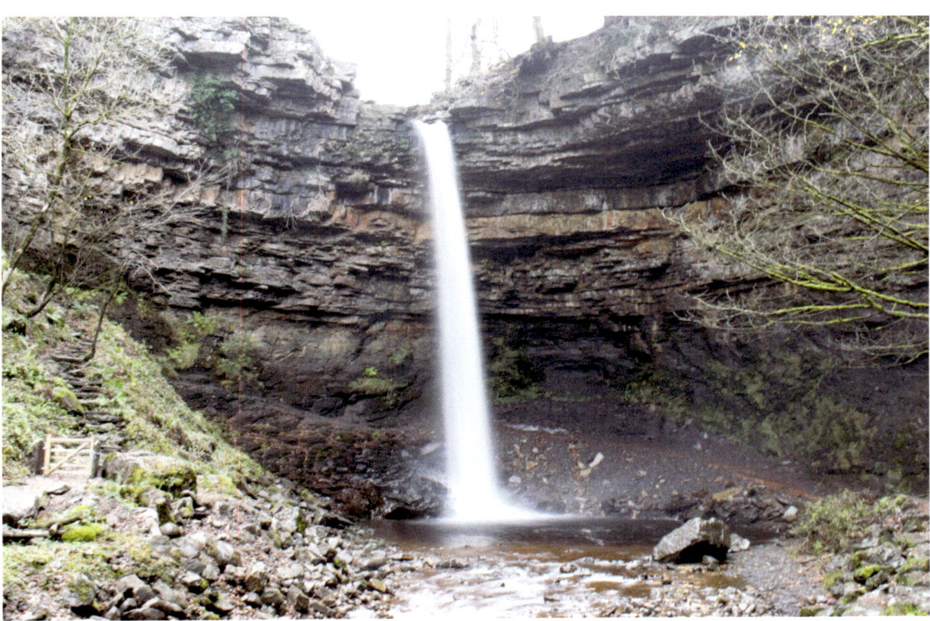

Hardraw Force was Robin Hood's favourite bathing spot.

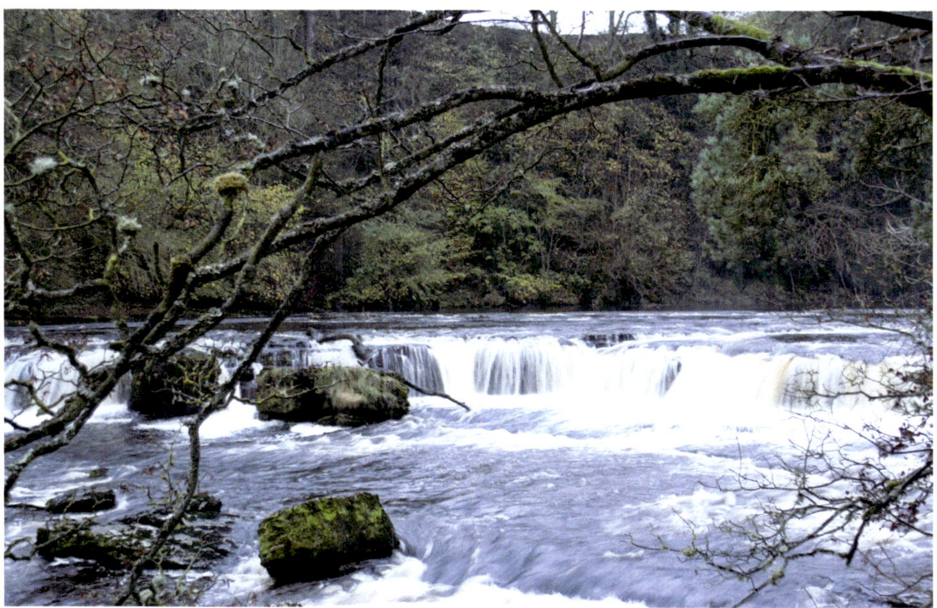

One particular documentary well worth seeking is Barry Cockroft's *The Dale That Died* (1975) – just head to the British Film Institute's (BFI) website, which says:

'I thought there was a great future in these hills,' laments 61-year-old Joe Gibson. 'I cannot see any future now.' Joe is an ex-miner, now scraping a living as a sheep farmer in Grisedale, a Yorkshire dale once home to 14 families but now farmed only by Gibson, with help from his wife and son. But Joe and his family's future on the farm now looks uncertain as the owner plans to sell. This poignant, elegiac film, directed by Barry Cockroft for Yorkshire TV, hit a nerve when it aired in 1975.

Grisedale is 8 miles east of Sedbergh in the north-west of the Park, with Cockroft calling it 'the most romantic dale in all of Yorkshire ... complete in its unspoilt beauty, serenity and vivid history'. The narrator, Paul Dunstan, is excellent too at setting the scene, talking about 'beautiful desolation' and 'soaring pastures', which had changed to 'crumbling memorials'. Joe certainly has an idyllic view of what farming could be like at Mouse Syke Farm, taking on 300 sheep after the end of his former employment and trying various other cash-making schemes, something his wife likes to poke humour at.

Sadly, we see his battle with the elements, lifestyle, and trying to keep the dale alive. He is heavily involved in Methodism, and there are some lovely scenes of the church packed with worshipers – but it isn't enough to keep Grisedale working.

As we get closer to the end, we learn that the farm's owners want to sell the tenancy, but Gibson can stay as long as he likes, providing he doesn't officially retire or die … a somewhat interesting loophole.

Joe's worries echo those of many farmers today. If the farm goes on the market, it would become a weekend cottage and farmed from the outside. To combat that, he reveals he would put a dummy in the window before he died to show he was still there. Then it could be passed on to his family.

In 2009, the regional daily *The Yorkshire Post* found Joe's grandson Matthew was still farming at Mouse Syke, whilst they also found the dale was undergoing something of a renaissance with people moving to the area. No mention of a dummy at the window though…

Food

Long before what could be considered exotic, in terms of ingredients, reached Britain, traditional farmhouse cooking ensured basic staples went a long way. Perfected recipes were handed down to each generation, with minor tweaks developing the taste, often dependent on what was available and where you grew your food. Take the somewhat bland oat – the basis of the diet in these climes because of its altitude and rainfall. Havercake was a stiff paste of oatmeal, water and salt, baked on a round portable iron 'bakstone' in villages around Wensleydale and Swaledale. Haver comes from the Old Norse *hafri*, meaning oats.

Further north in Sedbergh, Cautley, Howgill and Dent, haverbread was the oat-based meal of choice, whilst riddlebread was made from batter poured on a built-in bakstone in the area around Ingleborough and further south in Bentham and Bowland. Then there was clapbread and oatcakes, baked across the Dales, and 'tharve' cake in Nidderdale, a thick loaf made of wholemeal baked on a girdle.

The varieties depended on where your bakstone (or bakestone) was, whether it was built-in or portable. Many farmhouses had an internal bakstone made of stone or metal, fuelled by peat, bracken, ling, gorse, coal and sticks. The more portable bakstones or griddles were cast-iron big circular plates with handles that were suspended over a range fire.

The oatcake seems a marque of Scotland now, but the area still does make well-renowned food. Yockenthwaite Farm's award-winning granola, for instance, is vastly popular, whilst at Town End Farm in Airton near Malham, you can buy homemade Yorkshire chorizo, a Spanish-inspired paprika-flavoured fermented sausage. Yet, it's cheese where the Dales excel … from the well-known Wensleydale Creamery (TV's *Wallace and Gromit* propelling it to international fame) to the must-visit Courtyard Dairy near Settle.

Cheesemaking in the Park and over the border in Nidderdale is undergoing something of a renaissance. Historically, Wensleydale was a blue cheese made from sheep's milk, and there were several distinctive varieties. Swaledale, Wharfedale and Coverdale all had their own type of cheese and, until recently, goat's milk cheese was made in Ribblehead. Curlew Dairy in Wensley makes a traditional Yoredale Wensleydale from unpasteurised milk.

At Low Riggs Farm in Middlesmoor, Nidderdale, Andrew and Sally Hattan make an unpasteurised Wensleydale-style cheese, an artisan product that is best tasted when young. It is buttery, bursts on the tongue, and is made from milk produced from the pastures on the farm. As a result, the cheese is seasonal and reflects the changes in the quality and diversity of the grazing that is available through spring and summer. Silage isn't used – this is pasture- and meadow-fed milk which results in a denser flavour and a softer cheese at room temperature.

Andrew and Sally are first-generation farmers – the former's career encompassing farm management with CWS Agriculture, a PhD in dairy cow nutrition at the University of Reading, followed by three years as a farm management consultant. Sally grew up in Leeds before studying dentistry at Bristol University and worked in the NHS as a Specialist in Special Care Dentistry. They came to Low Riggs in 2007 and after three or four years renovating the farm realised they needed to diversify to survive.

'We took on the tenancy in March 2007, but it took nearly a year to move in because the house needed significant modernisation,' Andrew explains. 'We started farming with 300 sheep and continued the basic agri-environment agreement (Countryside Stewardship) that the previous tenant had agreed to. It seemed to be the most appropriate way to farm up here.

'Eventually, we built up sheep numbers to around 450 ewes. We brought in improved tups, tried to re-seed some of our grassland, used inorganic fertilisers,

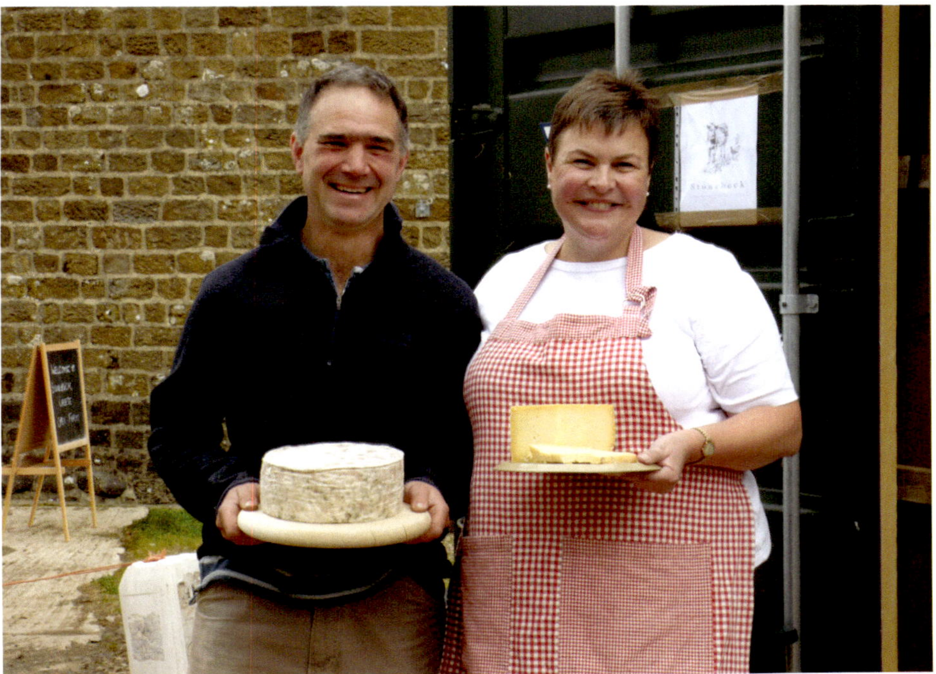

Andrew and Sally Hattan. (Low Riggs Farm)

and increased the bought-in feed inputs. At the same time, we were putting walls up, repairing the farm infrastructure, and restoring a couple of hay meadows. Then, we bought some Belted Galloways to help manage some of the rougher grassland. We tried to make them fit in, but unfortunately, they didn't really cover their feed and bedding costs.

'When we came to the end of the Countryside Stewardship agreement (2012), we did a SWOT analysis (Strengths, Weaknesses, Opportunities and Threats) on the farm business and realised it just wasn't working for us. We were constantly trying to compensate for the geography of the farm – its harsh climate, poor soils, short growing season and challenging access; we were fighting all of that instead of working with it – and Sally's salary at the NHS was keeping us going.

'That's when we realised that if we were ever going to produce anything from the farm, it needed to be 'of this place'. It needed to be low bulk and high value and produced without significant bought-in inputs. We mulled over what we could do and then decided to look to the past to discover what farms like this used to do. It was quite simple in the end: they kept sheep, a few pigs and a small herd of cows, and made cheese. They were subsistence farms in essence.'

Andrew and Sally knew whatever they produced had to be unique and command a premium. It was the only way the farm would work with the geographical parameters they were bound by.

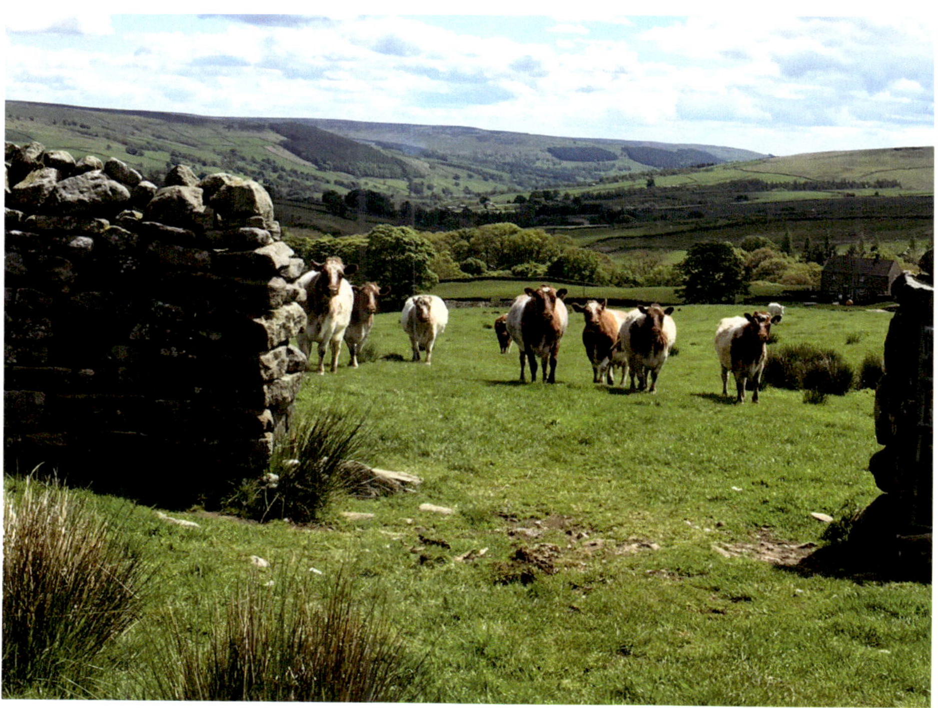

Northern Dairy Shorthorns ... (Low Riggs Farm)

'We wanted to produce a cheese that would reflect the land and the way we farm it. Therefore, it had to be made from raw (unpasteurised) milk because that required the minimum of external input and gave the maximum potential for uniqueness. We could then calve our animals in the spring and make the best use of grazed grass. We knew we couldn't make cheese in winter because it was too cold and wet, and we would have to bring in a significant quantity of additional feed to make the cow's diet good enough to produce winter milk. This would have changed the cheese completely and significantly weakened the connection with the land – "the terroir".'

The couple spoke to Andy at the Courtyard Dairy in Settle – a renowned expert in all types of cheese – and researched how to make their product taste fantastic and special. They experimented in their kitchen, using their scientific backgrounds to come up with the right mix and formula, and eventually opted to use milk from Northern Dairy Shorthorns, which would be ideal for the farm and its landscape.

'We knew we had to have unique selling points and the local rare breed cows added to that,' Andrew continued. 'We milk seasonally between the beginning of May and the middle of October, and are making sure our pastures and meadows are as ecologically diverse as possible. This is great for pollinators, birds and

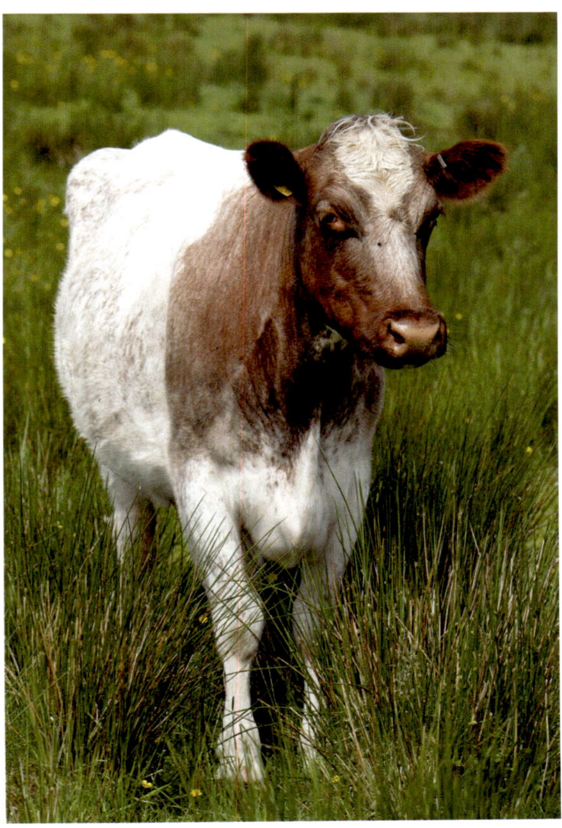

... perfect for the landscape!
(Low Riggs Farm)

wildlife, but also makes our cheese taste like it does. Our cheesemaking system also allows us to have a break in the middle of the day when we can do other things. It's a traditional, manageable way of making cheese and adds to our story.'

When you look at the ingredients for cheesemaking, you'd think it is a relatively simple process. The Hattans use just four ingredients – raw milk, a traditional starter culture, rennet and salt – to make their Stonebeck Cheese. However, it is the nuances of the preparation, the milk and the loving care that produce the quality.

The milk is gently stirred and heated to approximately 28° C before the starter and rennet are added. Once set, the curd is carefully cut with special knives, and the whey is drained off. That curd is then scooped up from the vat and placed in muslin cloth bags to hang for three hours to allow further release of the whey.

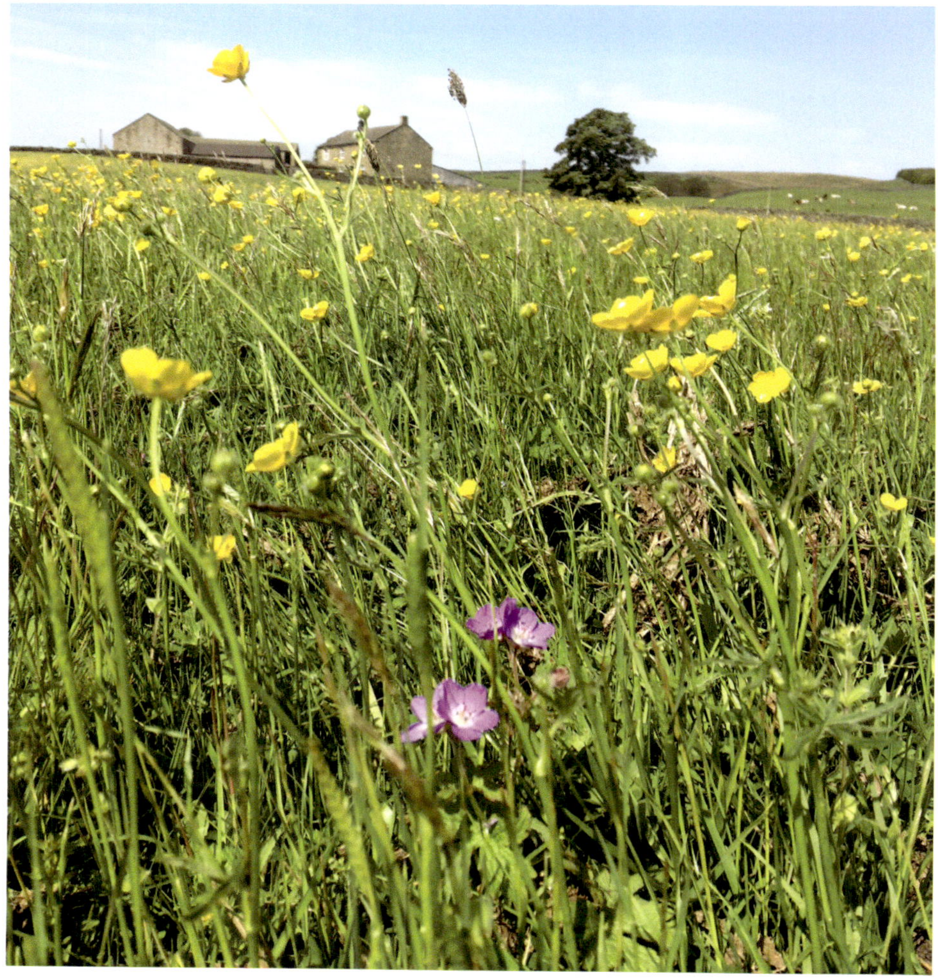

Rich meadows provide the ideal nutrition to create Stonebeck Cheese. (Low Riggs Farm)

'Our make speed – the rate of acidification – is slow, thus allowing the native microflora to express themselves and a creamy texture to prevail. After draining, a hand-turned peg mill converts the curd into small pieces ready for moulding. We then add the right amount of salt before the pieces are placed in the mould. After two hours, the mould is turned and then left overnight to drain. The following morning it is removed from the mould, wrapped in a cheese cloth and replaced in the mould before being pressed for two hours in a traditional cast-iron press.

'The next day, the cheese is bound with unbleached calico and hand-sewn with long-stitch before its final pressing. We then move it to our maturation area, which is cool and humid, so it can develop its natural rind and deepen in flavour.'

In 2023, Low Riggs produced just under 4 tonnes of cheese and their ambition is to reach 6 tonnes in the next few years. It sells out very quickly and is eaten all over the country in top restaurants and bistros. It means that the enterprise and the farm are now strong enough to support the family – a far cry from ten years ago when they thought long and hard about exiting the industry.

'We feel very privileged to be able to use all our experience and education to ensure this works for us. The cheese community in the Dales is such a special one and I think we're really fortunate to be here in such a beautiful place.'

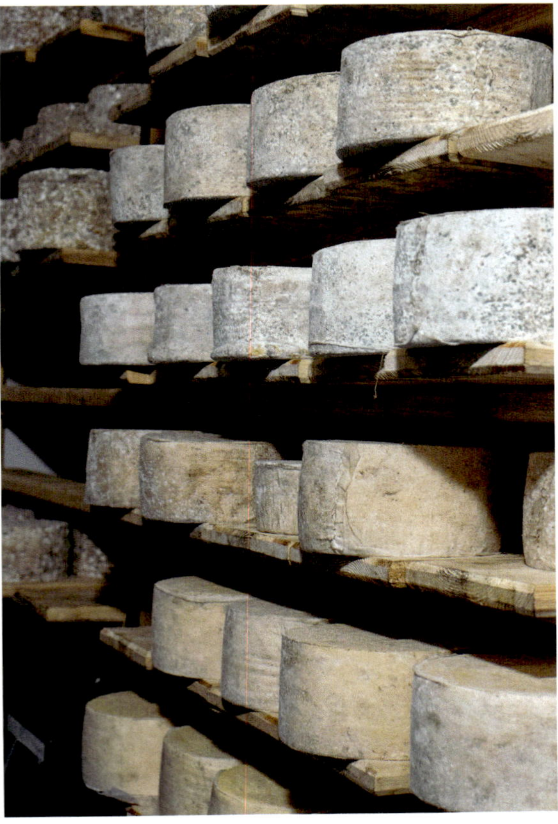

Maturing room. (Low Riggs Farm)

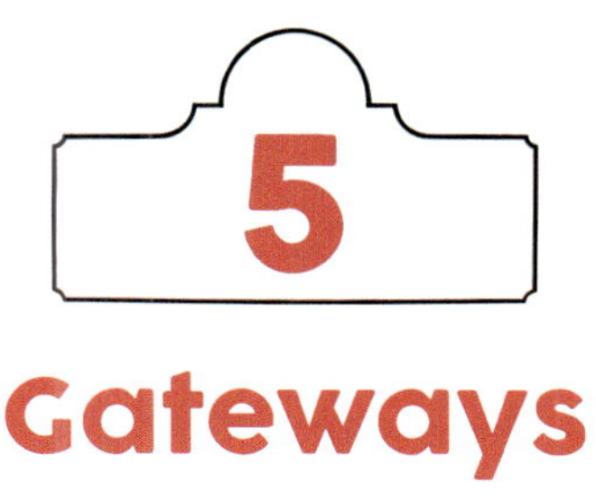

5

Gateways

Skipton

Skipton is the old capital of Craven, a market town that has recently earned the moniker of 'Little Ibiza' due to its burgeoning bar scene. It's a sum of its parts: a classic cobble-lined town with side passages revealing hidden pubs and shops. The Leeds–Liverpool canal is nearby, atmospheric alongside locks and peaceful meanders away from the main strip.

At the top of the main street is Skipton Castle with origins of more than 900 years. Robert de Romille built a timber fort here in around 1090, but that was soon destroyed by Scots who would raid northern England. It was replaced with a sounder stone building before Edward II handed it to the Clifford family in 1310 when Robert Clifford was appointed Lord Clifford of Skipton and Guardian of Craven.

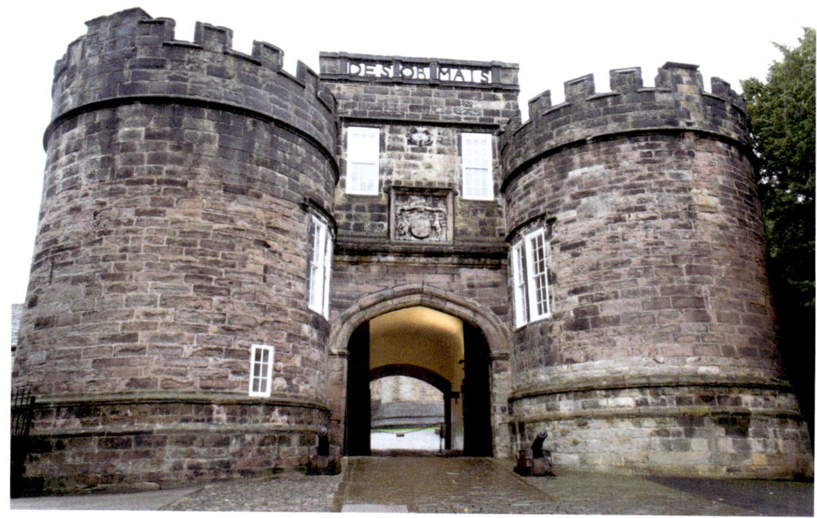

Skipton Castle is a dramatic gateway to the Dales – inside is a yew tree which was planted when Lady Anne Clifford restored the castle after the Civil War of 1645.

Robert began fortifying the site but was killed in the Battle of Bannockburn in 1314, with the job incomplete. It fell following a three-year siege during the Civil War in 1645, in which Oliver Cromwell negotiated. After the siege, it was restored under Lady Anne Clifford and the family's livery still flies on the castle as well as the yew tree planted in the courtyard to signal the repairs. The tree is impressive when it blossoms and is the perfect setting for the exploration that lies beyond. The castle is lovingly preserved in every way and open to the public.

Kirkby Stephen

When the Yorkshire Dales National Park expanded its boundaries by 417 square kilometres in 2016, it welcomed an already Dales-esque town in Kirkby Stephen. Nestled in the Upper Eden Valley, right on the edge of the Park's northernmost claim, it has historic buildings, cobbled yards and a bundle of places to visit in its environs. Nearby is Pendragon Castle, apparently founded by Uther Pendragon, the father of King Arthur, and the site of a Roman fort built as a stopping-off point between camps at Bainbridge and Brough. Evidence currently suggests otherwise … spoiling a good story … as the present castle dates from the late twelfth century with archaeological digs not suggesting anything else to the contrary. It was reputedly set alight by the Scots in 1341, before being rebuilt in the 1360s. It was beset by fire again in 1541 before Lady Anne Clifford restored it in 1660. She added stables and a bakehouse to return it to its former glory.

Less than 3 miles away from the town is Smardale Gill Nature Reserve which is well worth a visit for the differing birds, flowers and butterflies, set in the backdrop of the steep gill. It has species-rich grassland which includes bloody crane's-bill, rock-rose, horseshoe vetch, frog, fragrant and greater butterfly orchid as well as woodland that has been present since medieval times. It is also one of only two sites in England where you can see the Scotch argus butterfly, whilst green woodpeckers, treecreepers, ravens and sparrowhawks are resident all year round.

The reserve has 6 kilometres of level walking (and an accessible route) and, until recently, you could walk across the Grade II listed viaduct and see the views.

Back in the town, pay attention to the church of St Stephen known as the 'Cathedral of the Dales' because of its 'size and elegance'. The real highlight of the building is the 'Loki stone' – a bound, bearded devil who may represent the Norse god Loki. Information from the church says that:

> According to Nordic myth, Loki was fettered and tormented by his fellow gods in punishment for the killing of Baldur the Beautiful. The stone dates

from around 900–1000 and once also formed part of a cross shaft, though we can only speculate about the other images that once stood above and below it.

Inside, you cannot fail to be mesmerised by the high arches and beautiful tiled floor. It is Grade II listed.

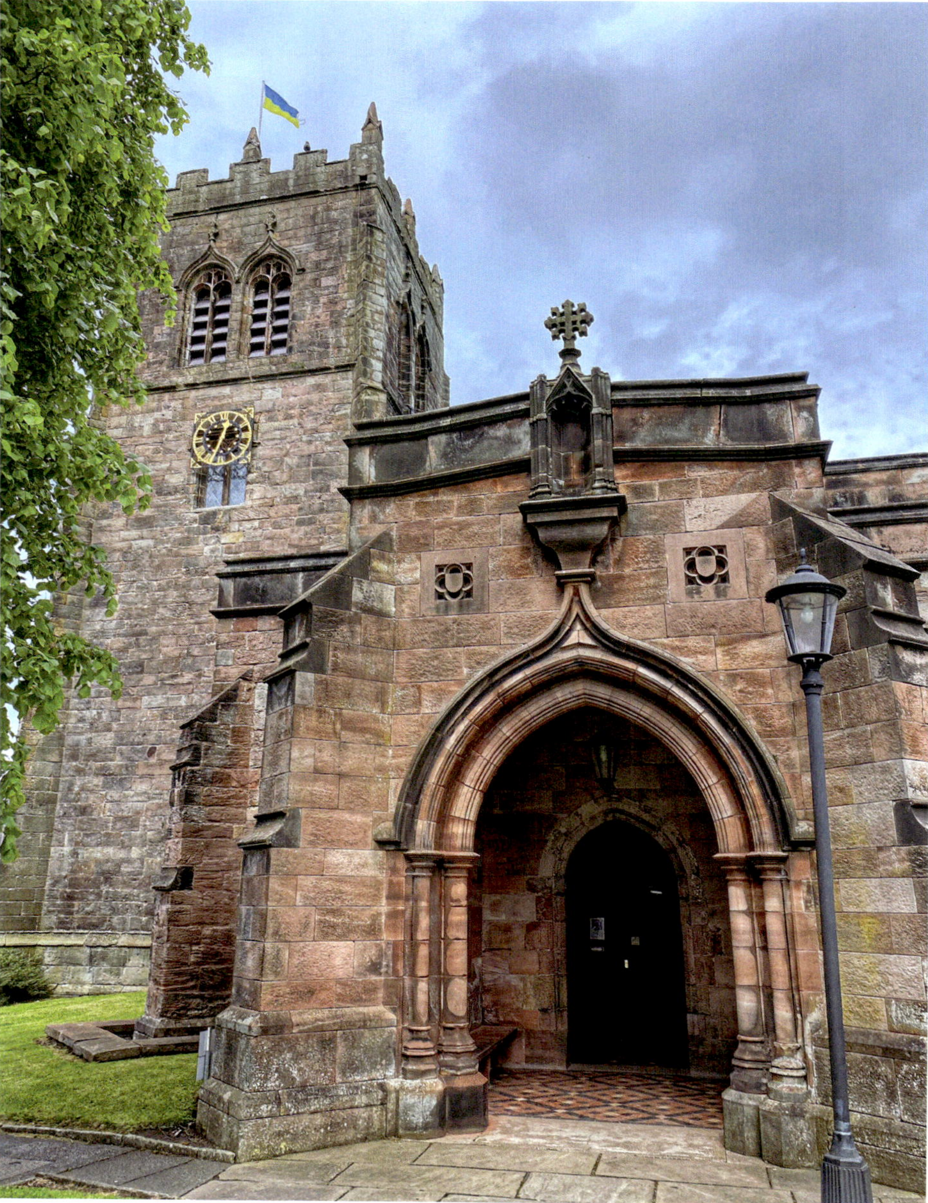

The church of St Stephen in Kirkby Stephen. (Johnny Hartnell)

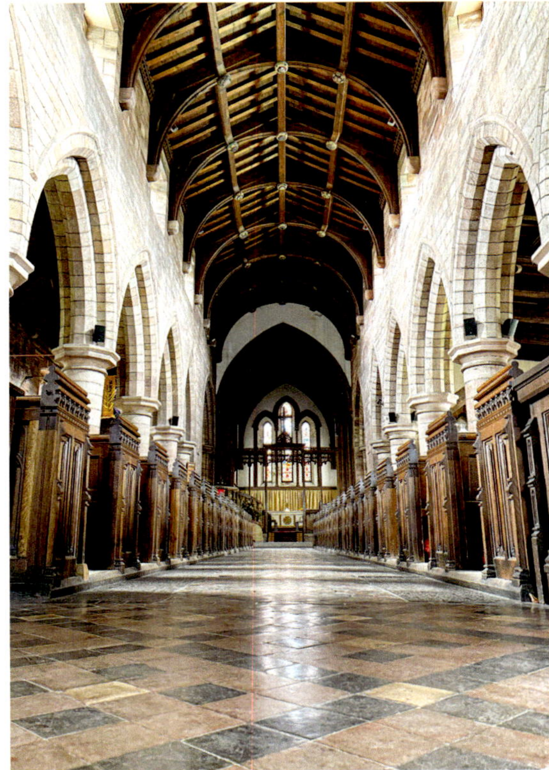

Left: The church has a stunning interior. (Johnny Hartnell)

Below and overleaf: Some of the fascinating artefacts and monuments on display. (Johnny Hartnell)

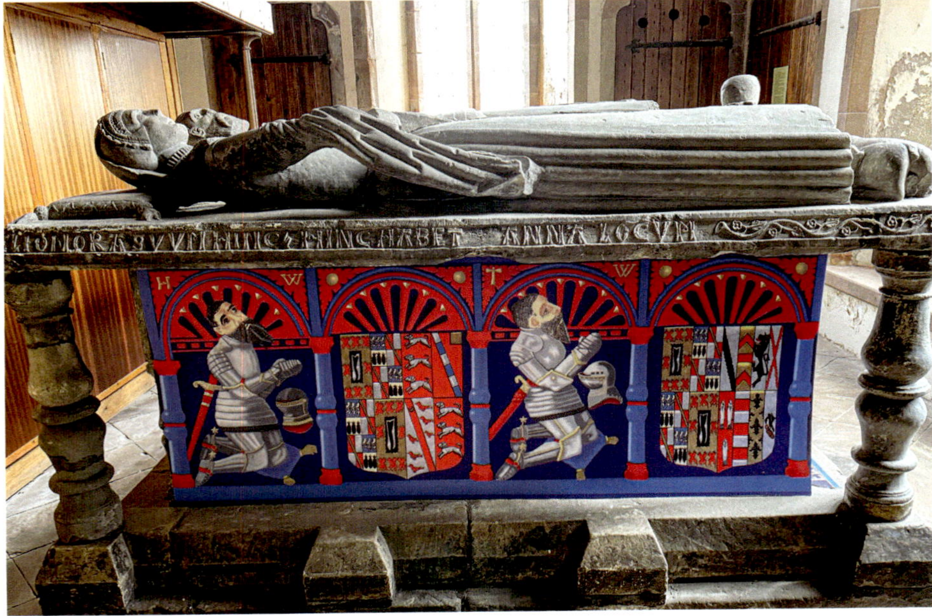

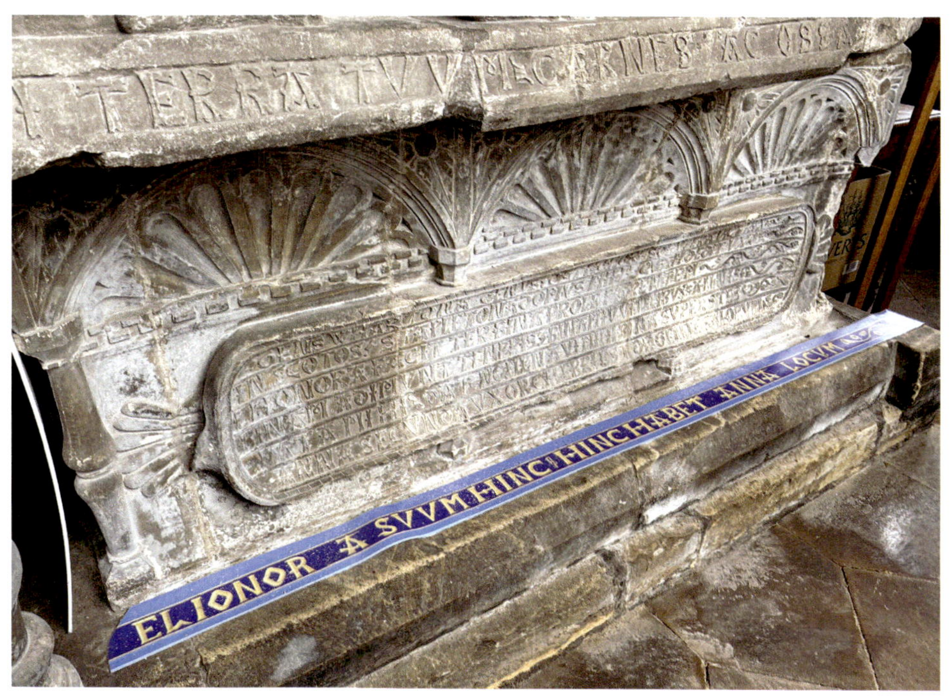

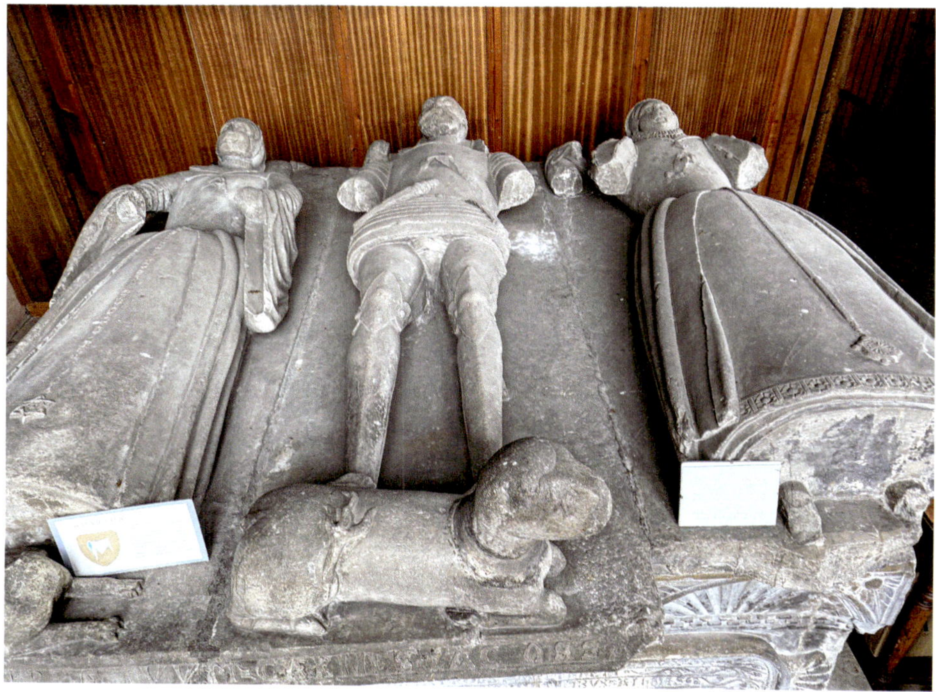

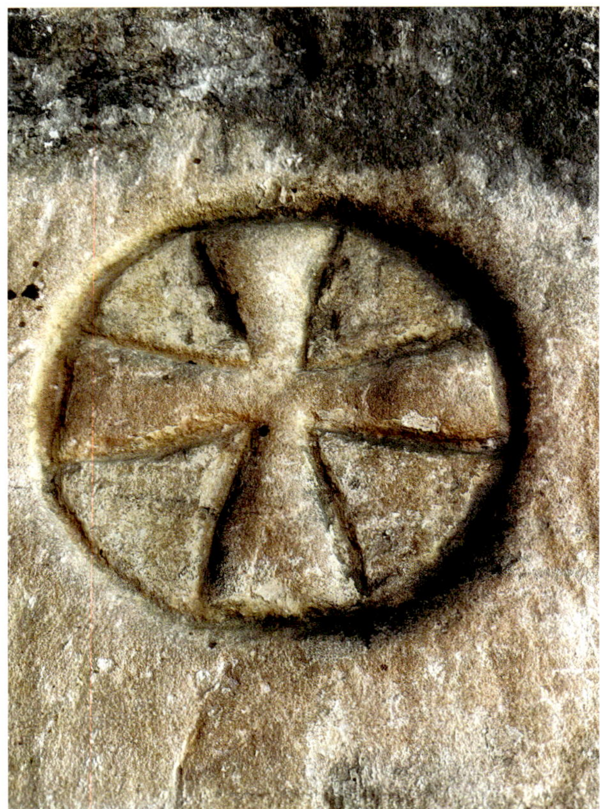

Pateley Bridge

Pateley Bridge has the quirk of being a gateway to two areas that have been designated for their beauty: the Dales and Nidderdale National Landscape. It's also a great place for exploring nearby reservoirs and gorges as well as a great deal of independent cafes and the oldest sweet shop in the world.

The famous Oldest Sweet Shop in the World has been trading continuously since 1827 and is officially in the 2014 *Guinness Book of Records*, if you doubt the claim. It's not just a title though, the sweets are made to original recipes too. Nearby are Brimham Rocks, Fountains Abbey and Studley Royal Water Garden – a World Heritage Site – and Stump Cross Caverns which is on the main drag into the Dales. The caves were discovered in 1860 by lead miners Mark and William Newbould and were opened for the public three years later for the entrance fee of one shilling. There is around a mile of passage open to the public at present, although the caves themselves are probably more than 5 miles in length, with discoveries continuously being made.

Tebay

More than the fantastic services on the M6 (please do visit and buy the cheese pie), Tebay is a base for exploring the Westmorland Dales and Howgills. It grew as a village because of the turnpike in 1760 and the railway more than eighty years later. It housed more than 1,000 people; a bustling centre of innovation until Beeching wielded his axe in 1968. From then it was almost forgotten, village life centring around the sixteenth-century coaching inn, The Cross Keys, and, in all honesty, most people just catching a glimpse of a row of houses as they do 70 mph on the M6.

The expansion of the Park gave it life, with the Westmorland Dales Landscape Partnership sparking projects to bring people into the village, recognise its heritage and, hopefully, in the future, a statue depicting its railway past. A motte-and-bailey castle sits nearby, as does a Roman fort at Low Borrowbridge. According to English Heritage, the remains of the 140-by-104-metre site are 'extensive and well-preserved. Partial excavation has shown the monument to contain widespread archaeological deposits which provide valuable information on the date and nature of use of the site. The monument provides important insight into a wide range of aspects of civilian and military life during the Roman occupation of Britain.'

Richmond

Alan Rufus began the construction of the castle that would eventually dominate Richmond in the 1070s and it remains one of the most complete fortresses in the country, according to English Heritage, with an impressive 100-foot keep. JMW Turner painted it too, it was the headquarters of the North York Militia and, during the First World War was occupied by the Northern Non-Combatant Corps, a unit for men who had asked for exemption from military service.

Wandering around the town, there's plenty to enjoy and many self-guided routes which you can use to take in its heritage. It's a town not without its quirks too, one of which is why the Christmas decorations include a parrot. It seems that the bird was bought as part of a job lot from Blackpool Illuminations many years ago, and it was the ornament that stuck with the locals.

There's also the ceremony of first fruits, an ancient custom that involves the presentation of newly threshed corn to the mayor by a local farmer. They then hand it over to a miller, who examines its quality. Once given the nod, the farmer receives a bottle of wine, and a toast is performed with others in the hope of a good harvest. I'll leave you to discover the 'Poor Old Hoss' tradition on Christmas Eve for yourself, unlucky blighter.

Inventions and Innovations

This chapter heading is probably a misnomer as these techniques weren't invented in the Yorkshire Dales but rather 'perfected' and crafted to make them a somewhat recognisable trait of the area.

Knitting is an obvious place to start, with the terrible knitters of Dent striking fear into those visiting the village. Locals would supplement their income by knitting stockings, and for the Seven Years' War, between 1756 and 1763, the government secured the 'worsted stockings' for the English Army that were produced in the village. They were of the utmost quality and could be made quickly. In 1801, it was recorded that an average of 840 pairs of knitted stockings came from Sedbergh and Dent. The 'terrible knitters', as they were known, worked in clusters and had a reputation for being great gossips. 'Terrible' refers to the ferocity with which they knitted but also the way they would rock back and forth whilst removing the loops. It was a job for all, with men knitting as they walked to the mines. Gloves and hats would also be made and sent by pack pony to Kendal and beyond.

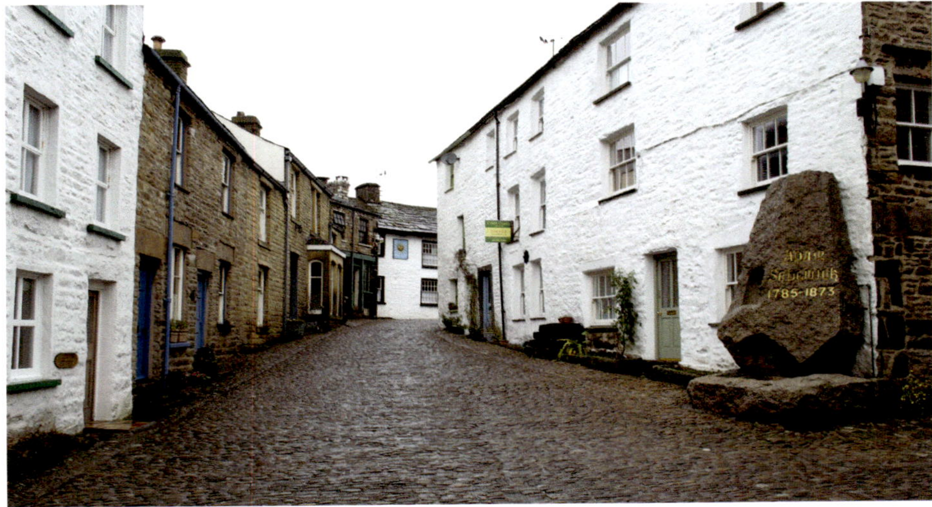

Watch out for the terrible knitters of Dent!

Kathleen Kinder's article for the North Craven Heritage Trust summed it up perfectly when she noted:

> The sheer hard work, organisational capacity, versatility and ingenuity of the Dales knitters and hosiers like Joseph Dover were the reasons why the knitting industry of the Dales was so important nationally, lasted so long and was so profitable for a few. Its success came at a price – on the backs of its skilled, but poverty-stricken workforce. Not surprisingly, when better-paid work became available, the hand knitting industry went into decline.

Dales' knitters were also proficient in the Midge and Fly pattern, which was a common design in two-colour knitting but took great skill. It was utilised on the palms, thumbs and fingers of Dales' gloves, and you can see a fine example at the Wordsworth Trust's Museum in Grasmere. Here, a pair of gloves is in a display cabinet labelled 'George Walton, Deepdale, 1846' and have 'G. Walton, 1846' knitted into the cuffs, making them the oldest surviving dated Dales' gloves.

British Textile History expert Penny Hemmingway (www.theknittinggenie.com) says:

> Midge and Fly is a slightly more sophisticated twist on the simple alternating of a dark and a light colour, called 'salt and pepper'. 19th century Dales knitted gloves often seem to have consisted of two patterns – one elaborate one for the more visible back of the hands, then a different pattern on the palms. The Midge and Fly pattern had the advantage of carrying but the dark and light yarns back round to the front of the glove, and doubling of the yarn trapped air, so had the practical side effect of making gloves warmer.

She adds:

> Dales knitters were nothing if not supreme craftspeople. So when you find midge and fly on say the upper welt of a glove, it will segue seamlessly up into the palm, and the pattern will be picked up and repeated, on precisely the right round, when the knitter got to the thumb, fingers or anywhere else. So there are no broken repeats, no messed-up motifs (as a rule). This is harder than it appears as, simultaneously, they may have been changing to a new and different set of motifs for the back of the hand. Earlier extant gloves are made from dark and light naturally coloured handspun. Sometimes, post 1860 and aniline dyeing, the dark natural grey or black will be replaced by a vividly dyed colour. One extant pair of children's gloves appear to have been pink and cream, which is consistent with colour recommendations in Victorian knitting manuals – where pink was perceived as a colour for both male and female babes/young children. Later gloves appear to be spun from millspun again in two strongly contrasting colours. Midge and Fly pattern works well with a strong colour contrast – like most 2 colour knitting.

The picture (below) shows Kit and Betty Metcalfe, whom Marie Hartley and Joan Ingilby wrote about in their book *The Old Hand-Knitters of the Dales* (1951). Kit and Betty were well-known as they 'used to sit on either side of their cottage door knitting cycling stockings with fancy tops. Kit used a crude winder and a sheath made by himself, and he knitted the fancy tops whilst his wife did the rest'. Both Kit and Betty Metcalfe passed away in 1904 at the age of eighty. They were married for fifty-seven years, having tied the knot at Hawes church in 1847.

Other innovations in the Dales included clockmaking and the production of black marble. The former thrived as a Dales' craft for several hundred years as skilled people such as silversmiths, carpenters and cabinet-makers would buy in parts and create a timepiece. They would then add their name and sometimes the town where it was made, engraved or painted on the face. At the Dales Countryside Museum in Hawes, there are several clocks by Askrigg craftsmen, but they are keen to point towards other towns such as Hawes, Leyburn, Settle, Skipton, Richmond and Gunnerside which had expert clockmakers.

In Dentdale, black-marble limestone was produced for mantelpieces, fireplaces and columns in the houses of the gentry. It isn't the most remarkable rock unworked, but when it is polished the white fossils inside create striking patterns. It was made from 1760 to the early 1900s.

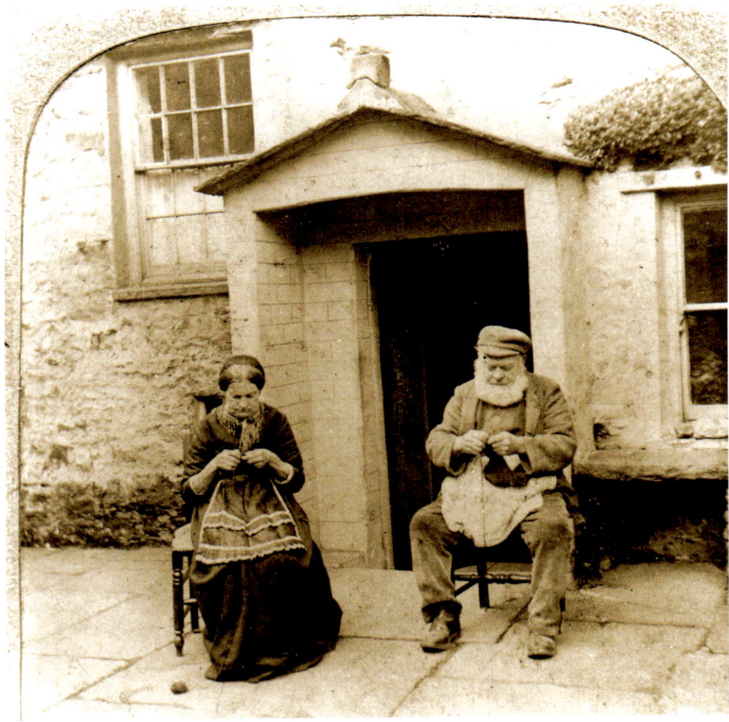

Betty Metcalfe and Christopher (Kit) sitting outside their house in Gayle knitting. (Dales Countryside Museum, Yorkshire Dales National Park Authority; courtesy of the Estate of Marie Hartley)

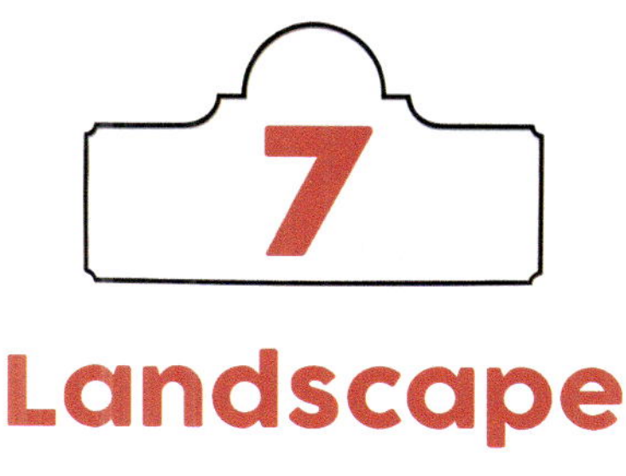

Landscape

One of the most special things about the Dales, something that should be celebrated, is its fantastic array of landscapes. It's been shaped by geological forces, worked and moulded over time as people make it their home, and now loved by so many. In 2024, nature recovery and habitat creation were the number one priority for the next Yorkshire Dales National Park Management Plan, with protecting rare and threatened species coming second and improving river water quality third. It showed the strength of feeling for the landscape and what it could deliver for biodiversity. It's not just the physical aspect of the Dales that appeals – the mountains, valleys, rivers and waterfalls – but the cultural aspect too. This is a man-made landscape, farmed, cut, gouged, fortified and enclosed. Here are a few things to look out for.

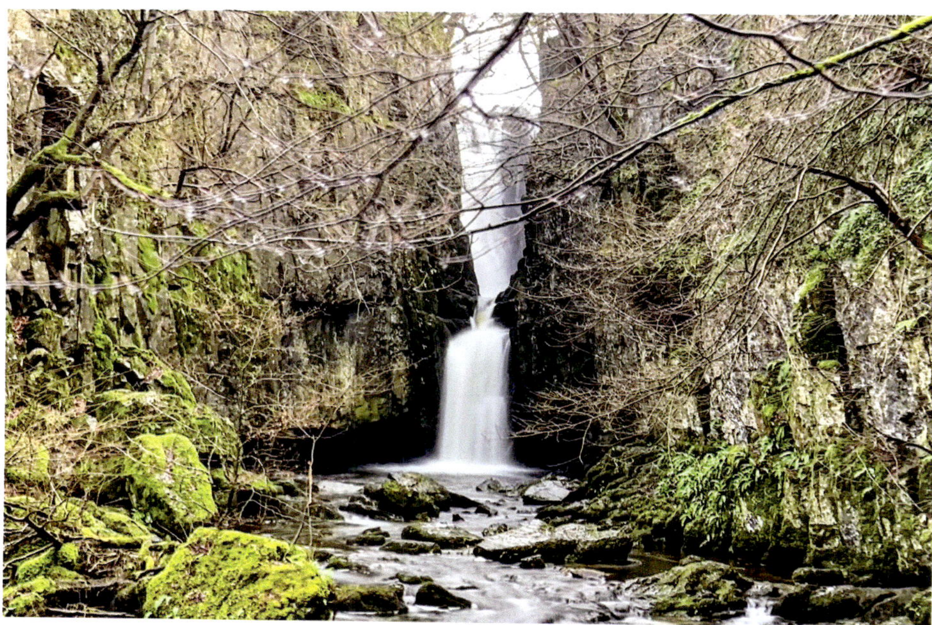

Catrigg Force – the Dales has some of the best waterfalls in the country.

Drystone walls, miles and miles of them, have been in place for centuries, helping to partition the land into regular, more workable portions. It began with the Enclosure Act, which was first passed in 1604 in the south of the country before the movement headed north. Archaeologist Dr David Johnson explained in his book *Discovery Walks in the Yorkshire Dales*:

Thousands of awards were gazetted in England and Wales with the bulk of the Acts being concentrated between the 1770s and the 1820s. Each township required its own Act. It was this Enclosure Movement, as the process has come to be called, that created the landscape we see today. There is very little 'natural' space left: it has almost all seen the hand of man. Once moors and fellsides had been enclosed, lime was added to neutralise the acid soils, drains were put in, and land management was introduced.

Farmers and land managers attempt to keep these walls in good repair, but there are simply too many, and most are returning to the earth. It's a costly business too; a good waller is worth their weight.

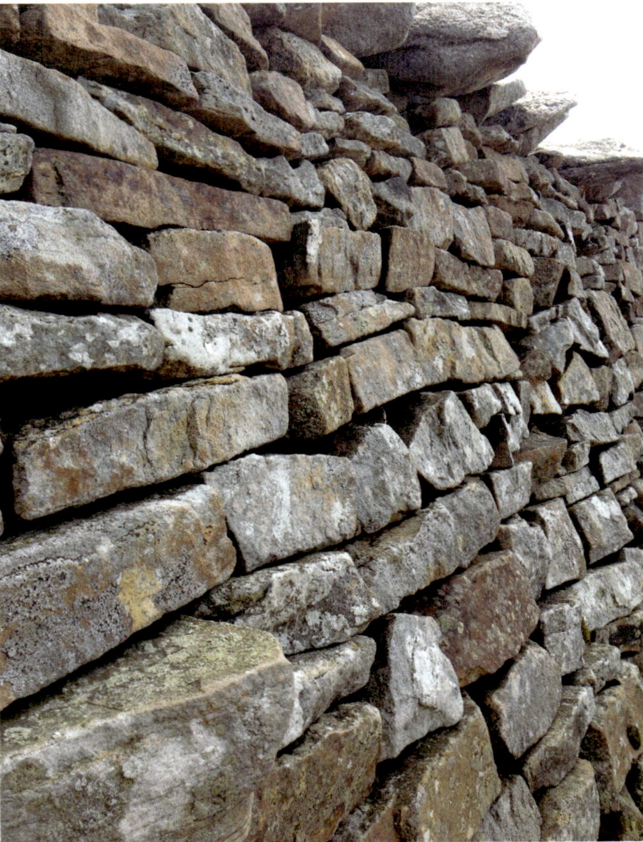

Miles and miles of drystone walls cross the Dales. They look great but were built to make managing livestock much easier.

In the pastures and fields, you will also find lynchets, pointing to a historical way of managing the land. These ridges weren't deliberately cut as terraces but evolved, as David writes, through ploughing:

> The plough of the day could only turn the soil one way so, at the end of each furrow, the oxen were walked back to start again. The effect of this would be to turn the soil only one way, and downslope had to be easier than turning it against gravity. In addition, the peasants removed any large stones, again downslope to the edge of their strips ... and thus the terraces came to be. Ideally, a lynchet is a furlong in length – a furrow long, that is how far an ox could pull the plough without rest. In width, they are a perch (or rod or pole). Multiply a furlong by a perch and you have a quarter acre.

Just outside the Park, in Bentham, is the Great Stone of Fourstones, a gigantic hunk of rock with fourteen steps notched within to allow access to the top. The views at the top of this 4-metre-high, 27-metre-circumference are incredible – this is an expansive vista, great for night sky watching and seeing all three peaks: Ingleborough, Pen-y-Ghent and Whernside. It's thought that there were once four stones, the other three likely to have been destroyed for other projects. It was placed here by a retreating glacier, although a local myth says it was dropped by the devil on its way to build Devil's Bridge at Kirkby Lonsdale.

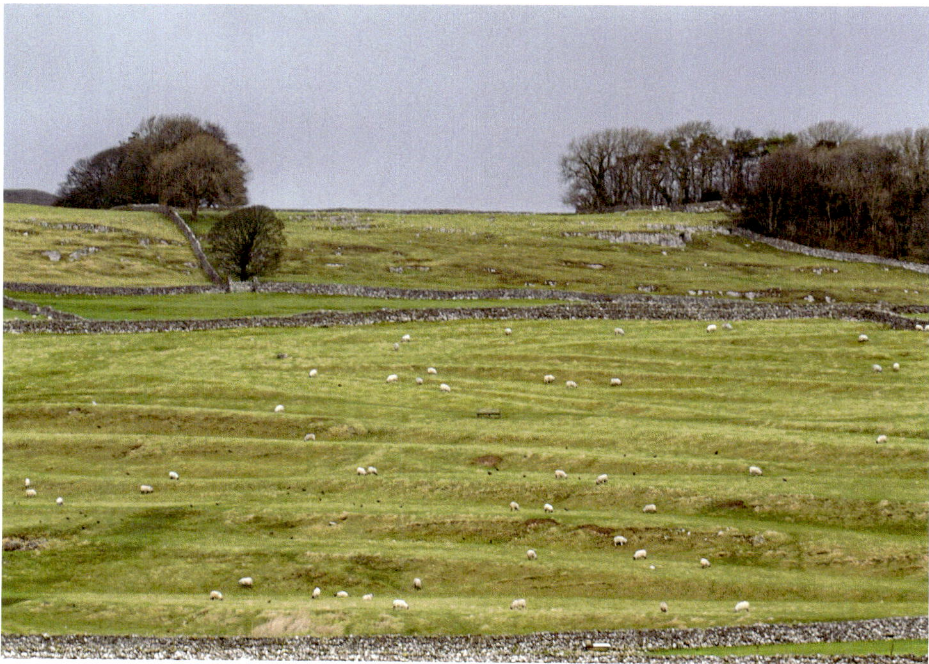

Lynchets point to a historic way of managing the land.

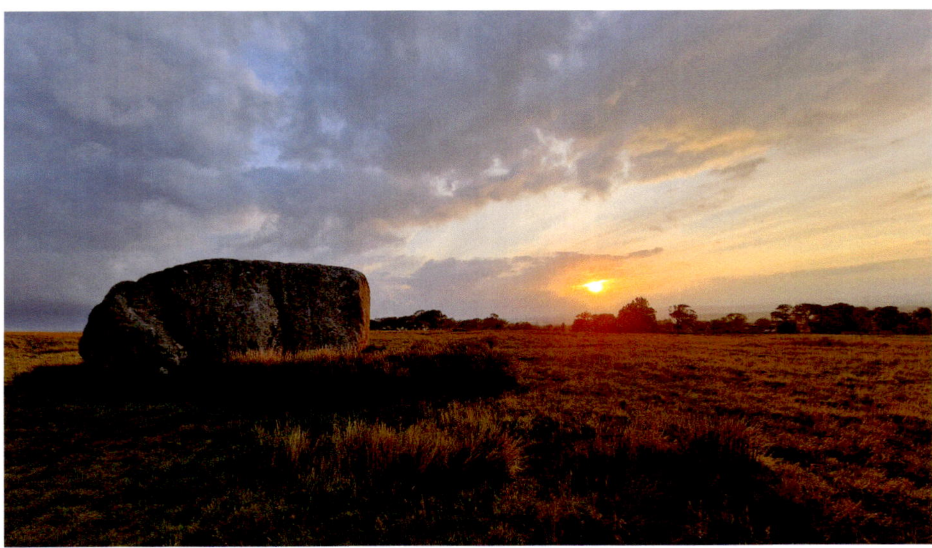

Above: The Great Stone of Fourstones at sunset. (Fiona Busfield)

Below: A Curlew watching over her brood near the stone.

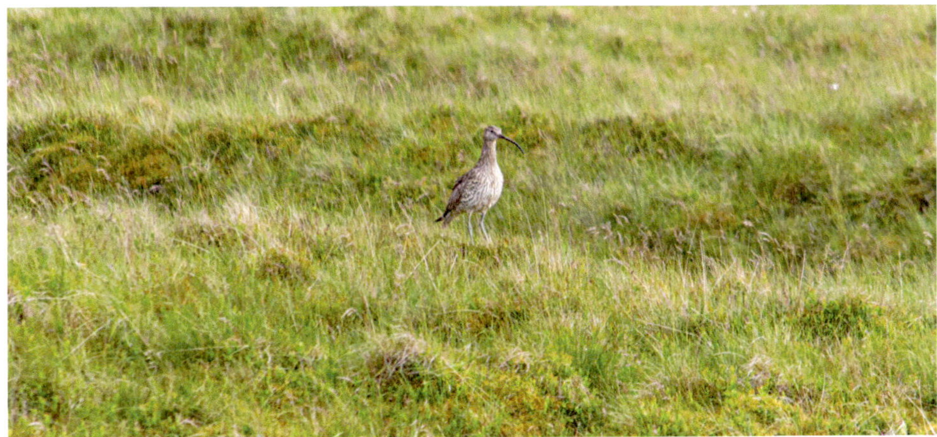

Returning to the Park, plenty of archaeology is waiting to be found. Because of the very nature of its karst landscape, it is difficult to plough. Discoveries at Kingsdale near Ingleton have revealed beaver and other animals as well as neolithic material. At Southerscales, an Anglo-Saxon settlement was found whilst evidence is still being collected on the top of Ingleborough. More than 1,500 new sites of historical importance have also been recorded in the Westmorland Dales following the completion of the first phase of an extensive archaeology mapping programme. A total of 136 square kilometres were surveyed, revealing several prehistoric settlements and dozens of new sites of interest, including medieval pillow mounds that are indicative of rabbit farming. There were also discoveries of

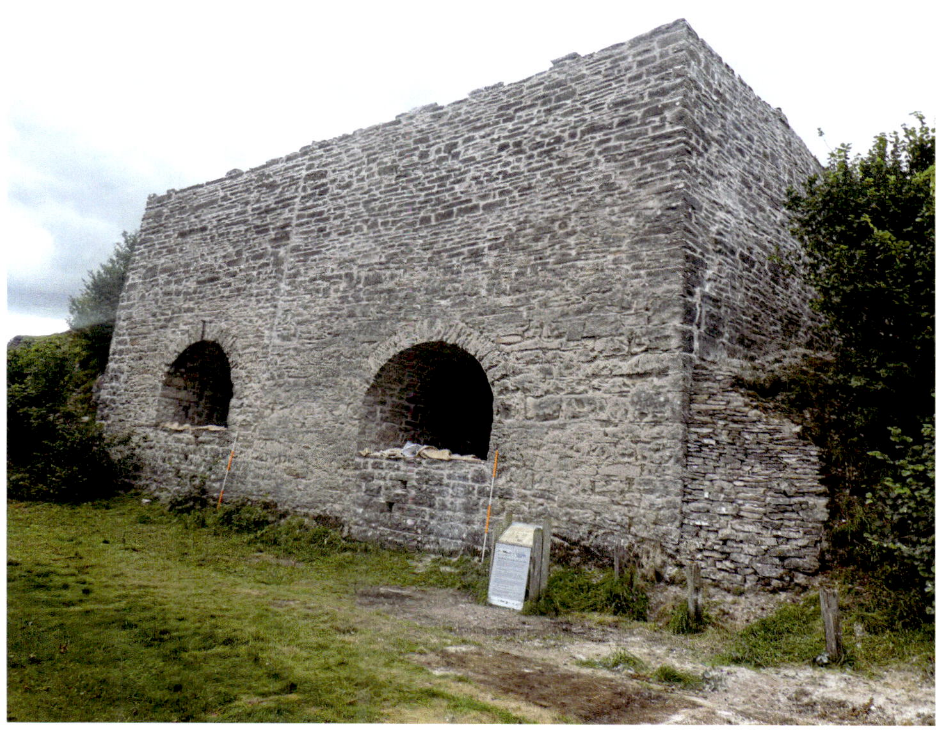

Above: The front of Smardale limekilns, which measure 10 metres high and 18 metres wide.

Below: The Smardale limekilns after their 2023 repair. (David Johnson)

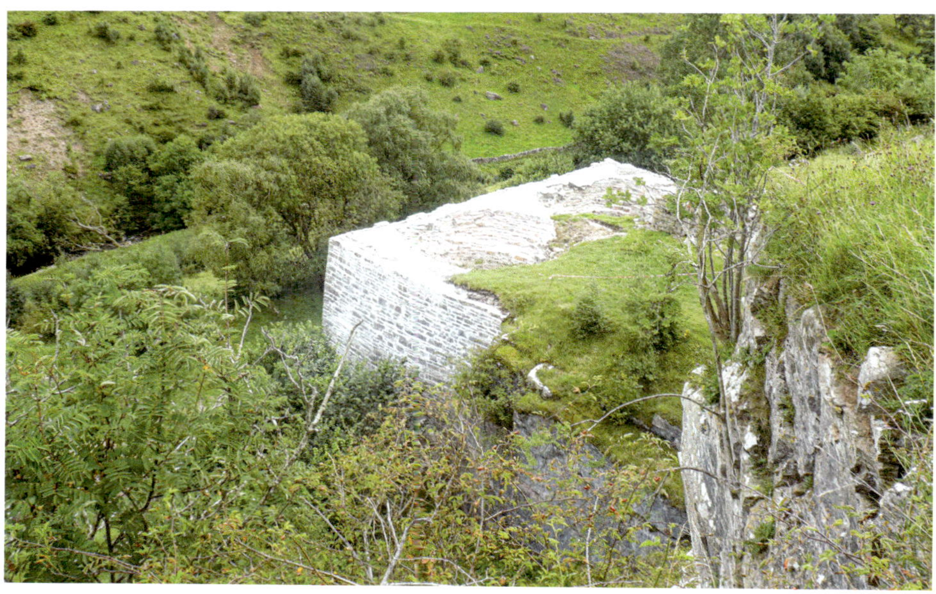

prehistoric burial cairns and enclosures, as well as features such as hut circles, sunken trackways and field boundaries.

Near Kirkby Stephen are the Smardale Gill limekilns which have been removed from Historic England's 'Heritage at Risk' register, thanks to a project to save them. David monitored the work on the site and said: 'It is a very good example of an industrial-scale limekiln and it's by a very prominent footpath in a National Nature Reserve, so it was worth saving. Stonemason Richard Staley created a bespoke device which was used to inject 30 tonnes of mortar into the rubble layer between the inner and outer walls of the kilns, to stabilise the structure.'

Other work involved clearing turf from the kiln tops, removing loose stone from the firing bowls, replacing badly degraded stonework, and re-pointing throughout. The kilns were built in the mid-nineteenth century and appear on the 1857 first-edition Ordnance Survey map of the area. Initially, they were built to produce lime used in the construction of the Smardale Gill viaduct, then for steel-making in Barrow and Darlington. They are part of a wider complex of industrial features, which includes quarries, railway sidings, an inclined plane tramway and an engine house, representing what was formerly a major commercial lime-producing operation.

Wharton Hall and Lammerside Castle are also close by and prominent in the landscape. Wharton is a fourteenth-century tower house with a gatehouse, internal courtyard and outbuildings dating up to the seventeenth century. It was built by Sir Thomas Wharton in the late 1430s, complete when a coat of arms over the archway was carved with the date 1559.

Wharton Hall is difficult to gain access to due to its location, but Lammerside Castle can be visited on foot from Wharton Lane. It is part of a much larger, fourteenth-century estate that was owned by the Warcop family, loyal to Richard III. They were eventually driven out of the area by the Cliffords and Whartons. Castlellogy – www.castellogy.com – says:

The castle formed an imposing complex of buildings, with the tower house in the centre, wings attached to the north and south, and a barmkin wall forming a courtyard to the west, with other buildings further to the south. Only the tower now survives, constructed of stone rubble and is 45 ft by 37 ft across externally, with walls 5 ft thick. By 1576, the area around the castle had been enclosed by the neighbouring Wharton family to form the Wharton Hall deer park. If still occupied at that point, the Lammerside site would certainly then have been abandoned.

There isn't a great deal of the site left but you're almost guaranteed to have it to yourself as this is a seldom-visited part of the Dales. Be aware … the ruin is known locally to be Castle Dolorous. Arthurian legend suggests this was where the giant Tarquin ate small boys!

Literature

Eminent archaeologist and author Dr David Johnson wrote in his book *Ingleborough* (2008):

From the time when the English gentry and minor aristocracy were prevented by Napoleon's machinations from undertaking their Grand Tour of continental Europe's cultural, historic and scenic splendours, the Ingleborough area has been firmly on the tourist map. It was at this time, 1789 to be precise, that the word 'tourist' first came into use. It not only attracted the political and social elite but drew in the literati as well. William Wordsworth came this way and, in his epic poem White Doe of Rylstone, composed in 1807, he introduced the reader to the family vault of the de Claphams, of Clapdale Hall above Clapham, in the church at Bolton Priory in Wharfedale. In Wordsworth's own opinion, this was his 'highest work' even though it was not an immediate success.

Twenty-seven years later, Wordsworth's friend Robert Southey visited Chapel-le-Dale whilst writing his seven-volume *Doctor* series – unfortunately described as tedious and tiresome by several unforgiving reviewers. The work focuses on Daniel Dove, with Southey's trip to the small hamlet vital research in establishing the young doctor's backstory.

Whether you're penning a dreary seven-tome epic or opining about the rolling hills and pastures, the Dales has always inspired creative people. Famously, Alf Wight – aka James Herriot – used his love of landscape, people and animals to tell his lively veterinary story in a series of much-loved books. They would be encapsulated in the TV series *All Creatures Great and Small*, which is still being filmed today. Other authors spellbound by the Dales include Clapham-based Alan Bennett and 'Yorkshire Shepherdess' Amanda Owen, who has written a multitude of books about running a farm in Ravenstonedale, whilst playwright JP Priestley called Hubberholme the 'pleasantest place in the world'.

More 'modern-day' writers include Alexandra Potter, who hails from Grassington but now lives in London. She has written sixteen books including *Confessions of a Forty-something F##k Up* which was adapted into a major

US TV series, *Not Dead Yet*. Then there's romantic saga writer Diane Allen, who lives in Settle and has penned upwards of twenty-five books. She began writing more than fifteen years ago whilst managing Magna large print books in Long Preston.

She says: 'I've always worked with books, and in particular library books, and I got to an age when I thought I'd had enough of running a firm and wanted to do something different. We were short of saga books at Magna and one night I thought I might write one about the Dales. The Dales was where I was brought up, I knew it like the back of my hand, so it made sense, for me anyway, to try it. I guess I was stupid enough to decide I could be a writer ... and I was proven wrong because the first book was completely rejected. In all honesty, I was a pathetic writer but a good editor. I've always been good at finding good books but in those early days, I was terrible at writing. Now I know some tricks.'

Diane stuck at it and her 'more successful' second book, *For the Sake of Her Family*, her first to be published, hit the shelves in 2012.

She adds: 'I was determined, stubborn and wanted people to know my Yorkshire. A lot of people don't get the proper Yorkshire. I wanted to tell its story within this amazing landscape. I wanted people to realise that Yorkshire is quite a proud county. I felt that was represented in some literature but in TV and such it was all flat caps and whippets. I wanted to put the record straight.

'My ideas come from history. My fabulous mother was nearly fifty when she had me and I was the youngest of four. I was always the one who stayed up late at night and listened to everybody talking. We were an old-fashioned farming family,

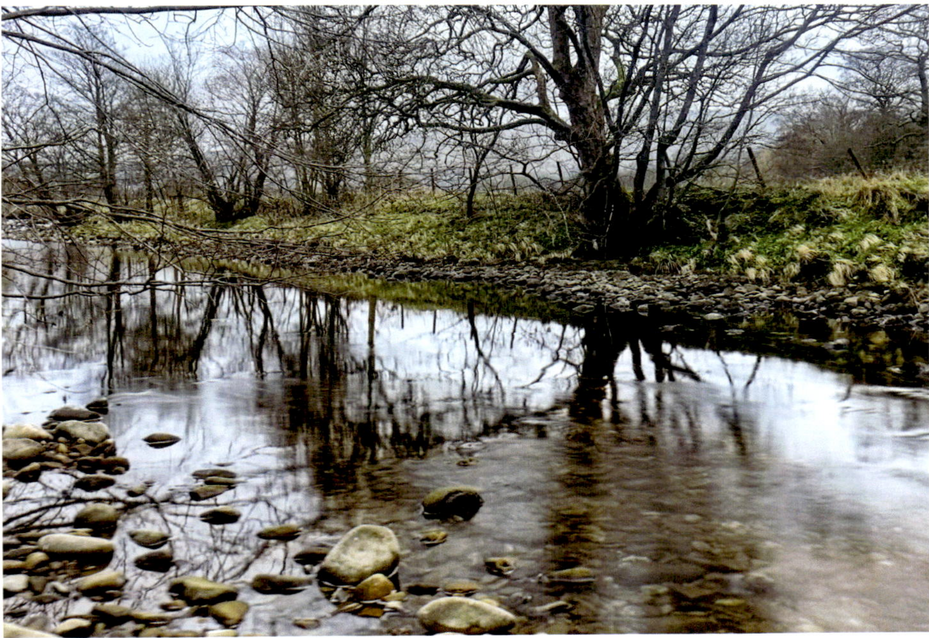

Diane Allen grew up around Dent, and with places to pause and reflect like this.

stretching back centuries, that met around the fire and told stories. My dad was Victorian really in attitude and this is reflected in my work. I never mention names in my stories, but they are based on truth and those stories around the fire. Yet, the most important thing is this landscape. If it didn't have the Yorkshire landscape, it just wouldn't be my book. I don't think they would work anywhere else. My heart belongs in the Dales; walking on the fells and seeing the flowers.'

Diane says her books are likely to be read by middle-aged to elderly women, but she has a strong male following who like the gritty realism of the landscape. Her readers are looking for sagas with a strong connection to the place they remember from their childhood. Her stories aren't a sanitised version of the landscape, and her characters reflect it.

'I guess there's a bit of me in my characters too,' she continues. 'Usually, the young girls are a bit like me; they're always fighting for something. The families are good families like mine, and there's always a good-looking baddy because everybody loves one. Then there's always the nice guy who hopefully wins in the end. It's probably a little autobiographical in places but my books are about a love and reading and a love of the Dales.'

Julia Chapman has a similar love of place in her *Dales Detective* series. She lives near Settle and has written more than fifteen books as well as having lived and worked in the US, France and Australia.

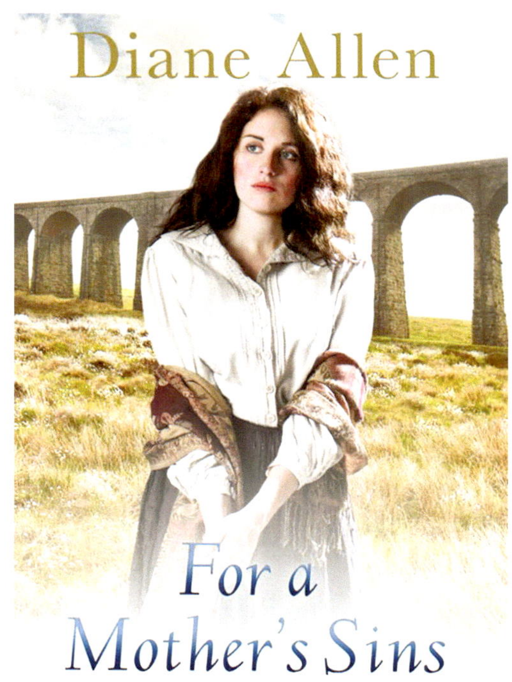

Right and overleaf: Diane Allen's saga series are incredibly popular.

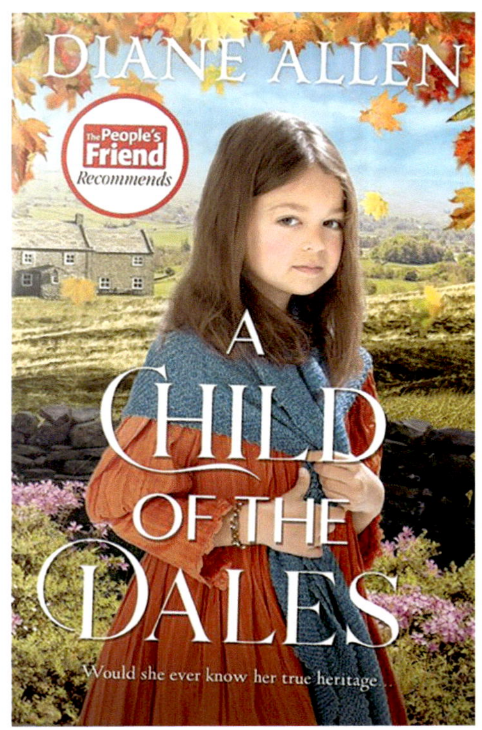

DIANE ALLEN
The People's Friend Recommends
A Child of the Dales
Would she ever know her true heritage…

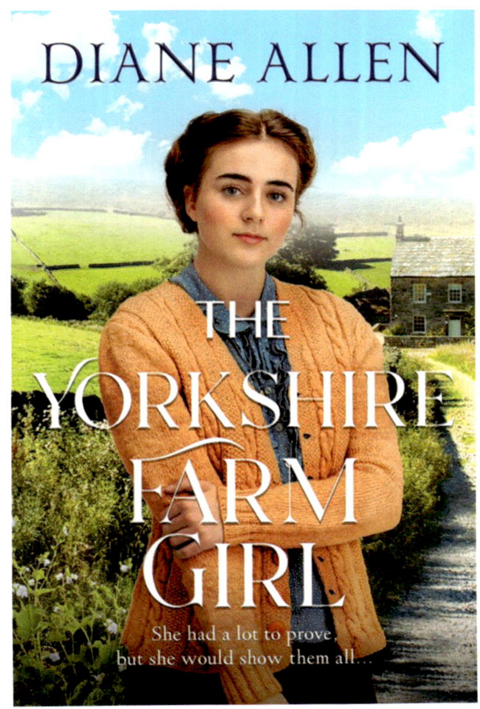

DIANE ALLEN
THE YORKSHIRE FARM GIRL
She had a lot to prove but she would show them all…

'The first series I wrote was set in the Pyrenees because I was living there,' she says. 'I'd received a rejection for a book that was set in Japan which said if I completely rewrote everything about it and didn't set it in Japan then they would reconsider. I saw that as a foot in the door but didn't know what to do with the advice. We were running a large B&B in France and looking out of the window I saw the view, the big mountains and a beautiful river and just thought, why am I not writing about this? The landscape had such a grip on me. I planned five books with overarching plot points across the series, but the main thing was the landscape. I'd never considered myself to be a landscape writer, but that had to be the most important character in that work.

'When we moved to the Dales, I would often go for a walk whilst mulling over plots. One time while on such a walk, I knew my husband was going to be driving past a certain point. Suddenly, I thought I would run to meet him and when I got there realised I'd enjoyed it. I'd never considered myself a runner but the next day, I went up on the fells for a run and now I'm completely addicted to being up there on the tops. It is where I do most of my work.

'When the French series was coming to an end, I was wondering what I could do next. I spent a lot of time running on the tops trying to thrash something out and was thinking "dark, gritty crime set in a big city". But up there, there's always a lamb, or a lark, or a crocus poking through; they were intruding on my ideas. After about three or four months of trying I just knew this was what I needed to be writing about but didn't want it to be dark. I don't see the Dales as dark, but I don't see it through rose-tinted glasses. I see the problems and I want those reflected in my books.'

Julia's books are labelled 'cosy crime' but there's much more to them than that. Set in the town of Bruncliffe, they're based in a fictional place that is anything but. Skipton and Horton-in-Ribblesdale are nearby; it's likely Bruncliffe is where Settle is, and Julia has a real knack for showing the Dales how it is.

She continues: 'I focus on real crime such as quad bikes being stolen and sheep rustling but always with that underlying robust humour that is so typical of people around here. The landscape was the absolute start of both of my series to date. I feel that places with different topography often breed a particular type of person. People who are isolated are hardy, resilient and pragmatic and these traits fit perfectly into the landscape and stories I want to tell.'

The *Dales Detective* series follows Samson O'Brien and Delilah Metcalfe as they solve various crimes across the Dales. Initially, Julia was awarded a three-book contract but had plans for ten in the series. Publishing is a funny game though and there's no guarantee three books, let alone ten, will make it to publication, even if contracted. Thankfully, the *Dales Detective* series stayed popular throughout with its plot-keeping readers hooked. However, had the series not been renewed after book three, *Date with Mystery*, then there would have been a real cliffhanger to the character's story. Phew! Publishing is a gamble for the publisher, but more so for the writer...

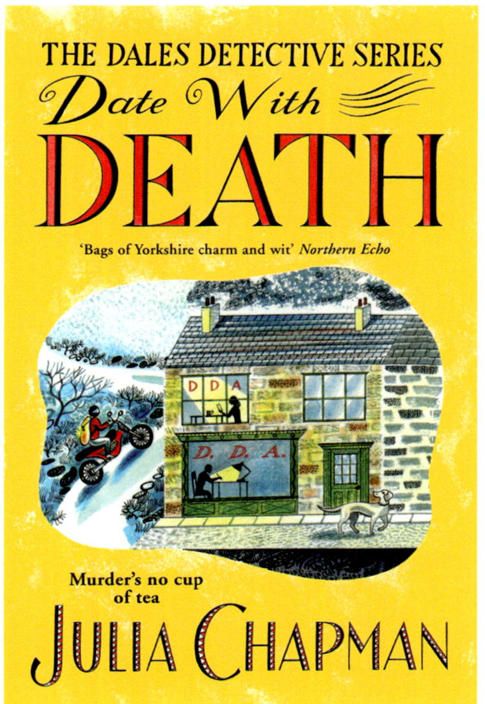

Julia Chapman's *Date with Death*, her first book.

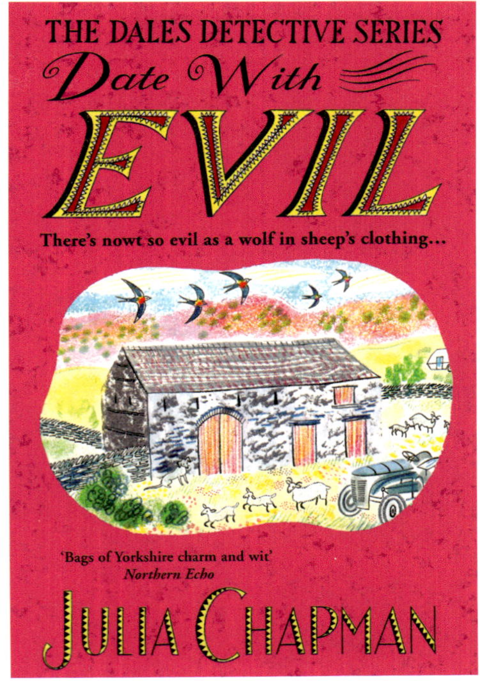

Date with Evil is her eighth …

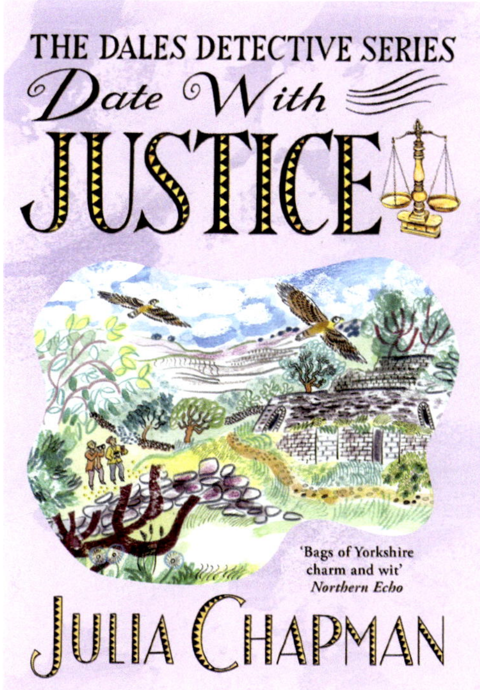

… Date with Justice her ninth and …

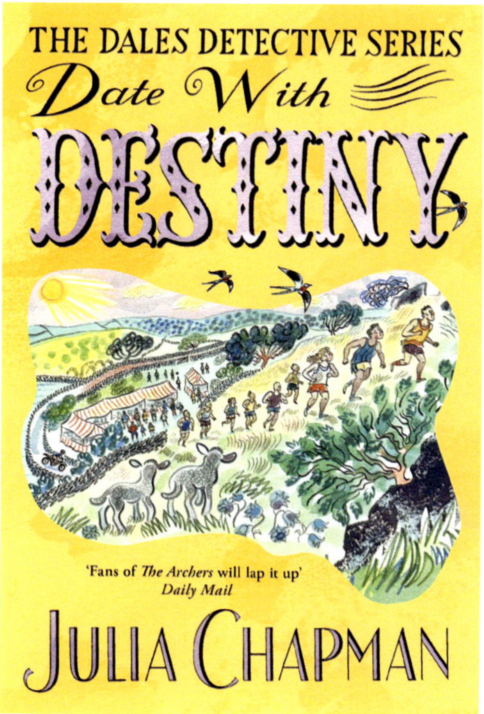

Date with Destiny, the series finale, all illustrated by the wonderful Emily Sutton.

Swaledale-based Susan Parry takes some of this jeopardy out of the mix as she publishes her forensic crime fiction books herself. Her work involves intricate crime, set in different parts of the Dales, evoking an atmosphere to the enveloping whodunit narrative.

She says: 'I did a lot of walking when I was younger but remember it being quite tedious as it was a matter of climbing up to the top of a mountain, standing in the mist and then walking down again. It wasn't very exciting, but when I came to the Dales it seemed a nice place to walk as you could get to reasonable heights, move along and then find a nice pub or cafe. I think my husband and I must have rented every cottage in the Dales at one point, and we fell in love with the place, particularly with Swaledale. As a result, it was always part of my long-term plan to come and live here. We eventually took early retirement and moved permanently.

'I started writing whilst was working for Imperial College. I always enjoyed it when I was younger before I moved into science. My father said I could continue to write as a hobby but getting into science was where I would have most success. I listened to him and read chemistry but when I came out of university, I couldn't get a job. I ended up taking a very short-term research post at Imperial College and stayed there forever. It was a very niche job as I was working on a very small nuclear reactor.

'Eventually, I got asked to do some forensic work and ended up looking at hair samples. I was also involved in a lot of soil analysis, effectively fingerprinting soils to match victims to where they had been found and traces of soil on boots. I also wrote a textbook and because I enjoyed writing it so much I thought I would try and see whether I could write a novel. It seemed very logical to do a forensic crime novel, it was just the sort of book I enjoyed. Then, because I had been walking around the Dales, it also seemed logical to set it in Swaledale.'

Susan says she never intended to publish the finished work; it was a trial to see if she could do it. Yet, around the same time she had set up a small publishing

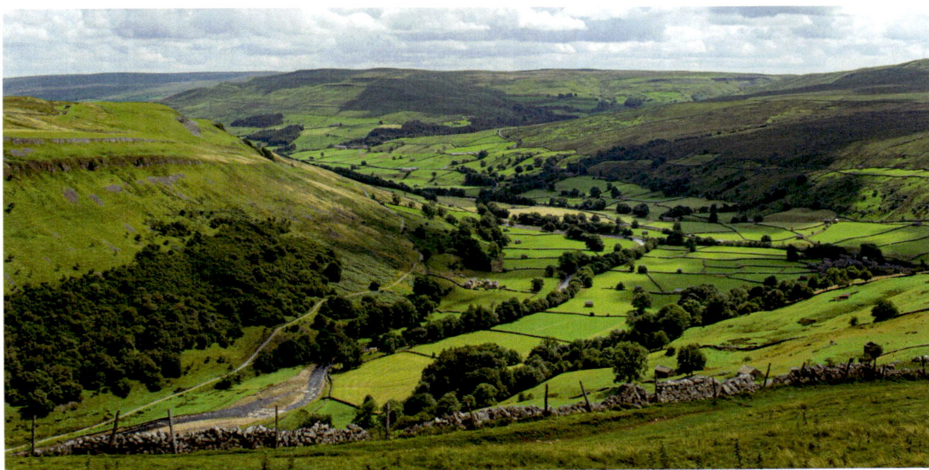

Susan Parry's first book was set in beautiful Swaledale.

company with a colleague to publish textbooks that had been written for students. Planets aligned; she published that first book *Corpse Way*, and a further eleven have followed. A new series started with *Tracks in the Dark* in 2024.

'I never intended it to be such a big series,' she continues, 'and I never planned what was going to happen in one book, let alone all twelve. I've been surprised at how well they've done but a lot of that is down to how I control print runs and where it is sold. I also have real control over the covers and the title, and that's important before I start writing.

'The places in my books need to be real as they bring authenticity to my work, and I like things to be accurate. I know some writers change names just to make it not quite like the places their books are set in, but they often are the places, and therefore it's even more confusing. From that point of view, I like to keep the places real, and my readers like that. I mention the pubs and the tea rooms for example but then when somebody gets murdered by the owner of a pub, clearly I don't want to use the real one.'

Susan says the places 'choose themselves' as the story makes its progression around the Dales. Her first book looked at the industrial archaeology of the lead mines, but subsequent stories have focused on the poisoning of raptors, illegal abattoirs and the Tour de France that traversed across Yorkshire in 2014.

She adds: 'I don't think my books could work anywhere else, particularly the first series. The main character came to the Dales, loved it and stayed there, much like me. In my new series, the characters were placed in Hawes, but the events could have happened elsewhere. However, it wouldn't seem the same, somehow. I've had messages from readers that show they like places I refer to and the landscape. It gives them a sense of belonging and connection and I think that is what all writers in this place are trying to do.'

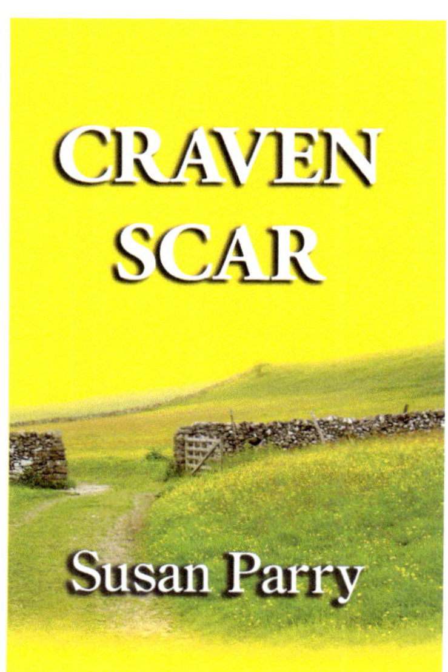

Susan Parry has written several books including *Craven Scar* …

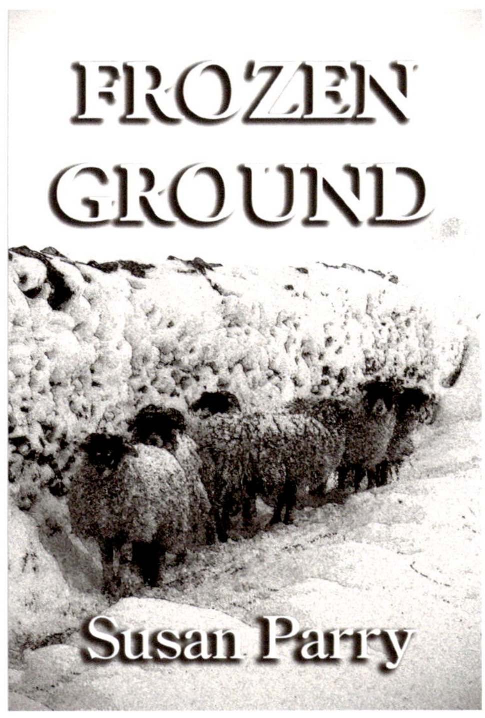

… Frozen Ground …

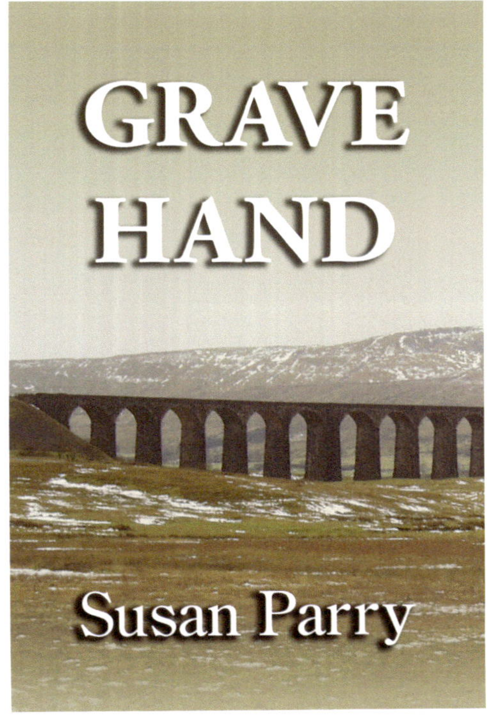

… Grave Hand …

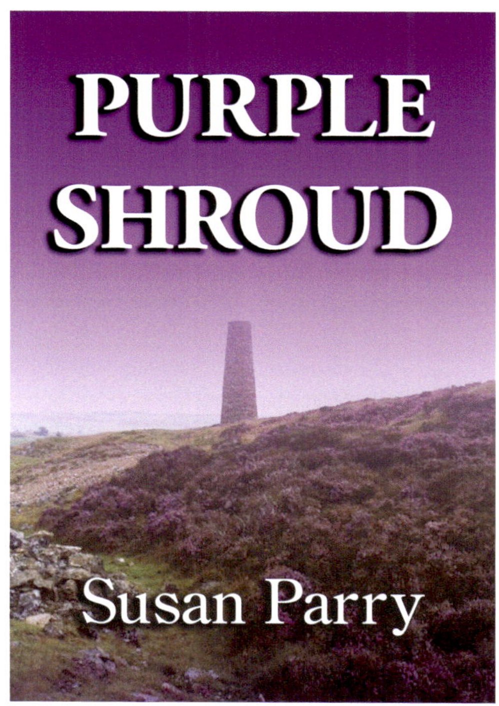

… Purple Shroud …

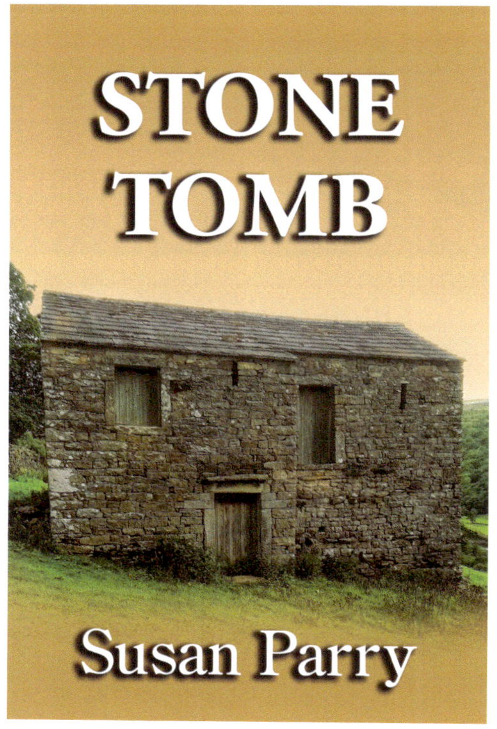

And *Stone Tomb*.

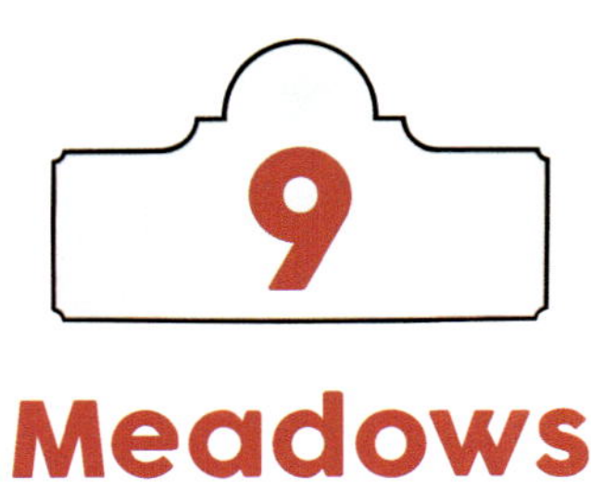

Meadows

The countryside is under pressure from several competing challenges. It is expected to provide food, sequester carbon, provide recreation, and be a home for nature alongside sustaining a local population and all the social and economic traits it brings. Managers of the land are often caught right in the middle of that debate with government, the public, the third sector and campaign groups all wanting a say on how they should farm. Consequently, economic policy, land management schemes and subsidies greatly impact the type of landscape you get. In National Parks, this is even more prevalent; these oases of natural beauty have to deliver a working landscape that is a breathing space for all.

We don't always get it right ... the intricacies of the Common Agricultural Policy encouraged farmers to increase stocking densities, which realised a decent financial return but led to intensification and a change in management. It's not completely the fault of the farmer, but rather the environment curated for them for their business to survive.

Yet, one of the impacts of more livestock is the fact that only 3 per cent of Britain's semi-natural grasslands remain. The traditional meadow, thriving with diverse, colourful flowers and other species, has been replaced by quick-growing grasses that can be cut three or more times a year for winter fodder. That's less food for pollinators, fewer species for habitats, and a downturn in invertebrates.

It wasn't always like this. In the Dales, some farmers are trying to buck the trend and are hefted to the meadow – and are making them economically viable too. Malham's Neil Heseltine is one land manager who is continuing the work of Walter Umpleby at Newhouse Farm, just outside the village. Walter managed the farm from January 1954 to December 1996, nearly an uninterrupted forty-three years working with the seasons and utilising what his animals provided ... muck.

Walter's rejection of modern farming methods was laid bare in his remarkable diaries. Now residing with the National Trust, his notes depict all the stresses of farming, from its monotony through to everyday life. He gave his diaries to the National Trust when he left the farm, but only after he had painstakingly transcribed and abridged them from the original. Considering there are two hefty tomes that contained his thoughts, there can't have been much editing. His first entry reads: 'Jan 1, Rate man came to measure up house. Injected Morphet cow for second time'. His final: 'Dec 16, Newhouses, Owen and Margaret and Roy Newhouse came to help me move to the Bugalow [sic] Hellifield'.

Much of the diary details mundane but important work such as walling, visits from the 'ministry man', dozens upon dozens of eggs making their way around Malham and various issues around the house. He also had a real penchant for shooting things in the early years, often for vermin control but a great deal for food. Haytime was the most important part of life and, over five decades, followed a regular pattern, beginning in late June to early July and finishing two to three weeks later. In only a few entries do we see it starting in August – albeit likely a weather issue rather than a shift in climate.

Towards the end of his tenure, the diaries take a sombre but understandable tone. In 1991, he lost his wife, and five years later, the farm was sold. Walter's life has changed over these years; he has much more help with day-to-day tasks and bakes a lot of pies to keep himself busy. In the final few months, it's sad to read about the sale of his belongings and the euthanisation of his cat and dog. It's the dismantling of a lifestyle, a calling to this land.

Walter's legacy was to leave a farm full of floral diversity and a fine example of a special and once-prevalent upland habitat. It is now a National Nature Reserve, a Site of Special Scientific Interest, and part of the Pennine Dales Hay Meadows Special Area of Conservation. It's a daunting task for Neil, who has been continuing its management since 2019.

'I can't take any credit for this,' he says. 'It's all Walter. He stuck to his guns from the onset and continued farming in the same way even in the '80s and '90s when everybody else intensified. It worked for him and the land, and you now have this amazing haven for wildlife and nature. To be honest, it is quite easy to continue Walter's work because it is all set before you. The meadows are relatively simple in terms of the management. There's never any sheep on this site, and as long as the other animals are taken off at the right time, nature can do its thing.'

Neil says the pastures are slightly different in terms of management and that he is still finding his way to ensure they work for his livestock and biodiversity. There are also breeding waders such as curlew on the farm, and it is vitally important that they are not disturbed, as a red list species. But the work of Walter and Neil is clear to see. This is a diverse meadow with key species and is buzzing with pollinators alongside vertebrates and other small mammals. It feels like everything is in balance, so it begs the question, why aren't more farmers following suit?

'Meadows have been replaced by higher-yielding grass species and the resultant change in management,' Neil explains. 'Even though the grass these traditional meadows produce may be more nutritious, they aren't seen as a high-yielding crop. High-yielding grasses mean you can get more grass from them and feed more animals, which I guess makes that system more productive, as you can produce more meat.

'Wildflower meadows are extremely diverse in what they bring, but I think this kind of meadow is seen by some farmers as a bit "airy fairy" because it's about flowers and pollinators and not about "real" production. I think this diversity of botanical species gives the animals a healthier crop. Let's be honest; we need the stuff that's in this meadow to make the world go round. We have to ensure a way of life that is as diverse as possible. We need opportunities for pollinators and plants to be diverse – as well as improving the soil. We're trying to do our small bit with regards to that, and it works for us economically, both financially and with our time.'

He adds: 'I don't think there's an understanding from the people who buy our products of how they are farmed. There's still a feeling that animals eat grass, and it's just grass that grows. I'm not sure there's a real understanding of how farming has transitioned into a very different beast from what it was many years ago. These types of traditional hay meadows would have been right across the country with species that grew naturally in those areas. When you read that 97 per cent have gone, that's bound to have an impact on biodiversity across the country. That's why nature is in the state it's in. Hay meadows are a part of it, but you also have an 85 per cent loss of wetlands as land was drained for food production. Something has to change.'

Campaign groups and the government hope that change will come with the new Environmental Land Management schemes and revamped Sustainable Farming Incentive. Public money for public goods is important – with tangible benefits for the environment – but the justification for any increased spending will come against other pressures on the Treasury. Then, these schemes need to deliver for farmers too.

'Our farming system delivers environmental benefits and puts food on people's tables,' Neil adds. 'We're in a better place now as we don't farm intensively, and we're in a better place with habitat and nature. I would like farmers to follow what we have done, but I know from experience it is difficult to change. However, we know the basic payment has gone, and I feel that in the uplands, if people continue to farm in the way they currently are, then there won't be many farmers left here. They have to change to ensure they survive and to be honest, that's kind of where we were before we made our change. We need to take people along with us to show that this kind of management is not only going to be beneficial for climate and nature, but it's also going to be beneficial for farming and farmers.'

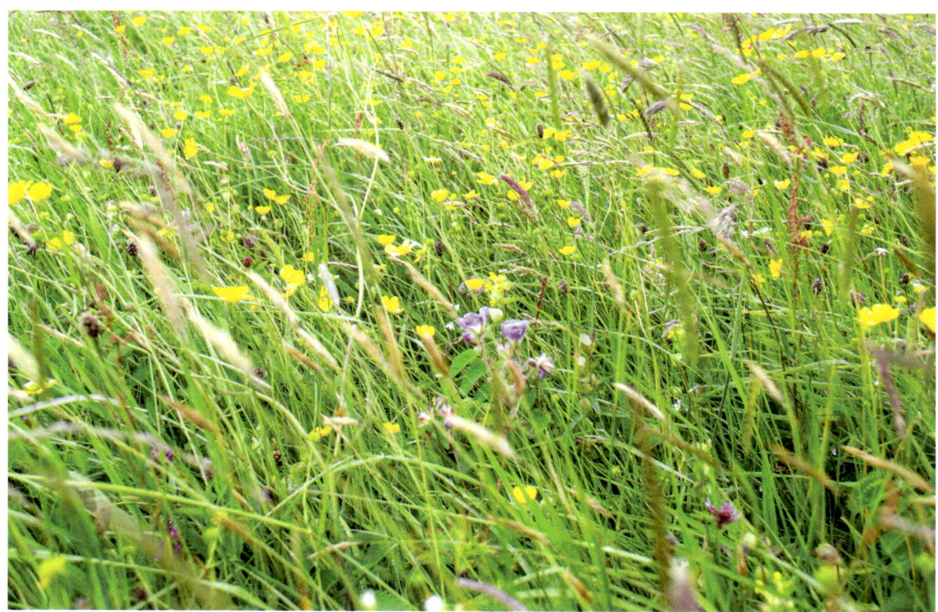

Above, below and overleaf: The meadows at Newhouse are impressive.

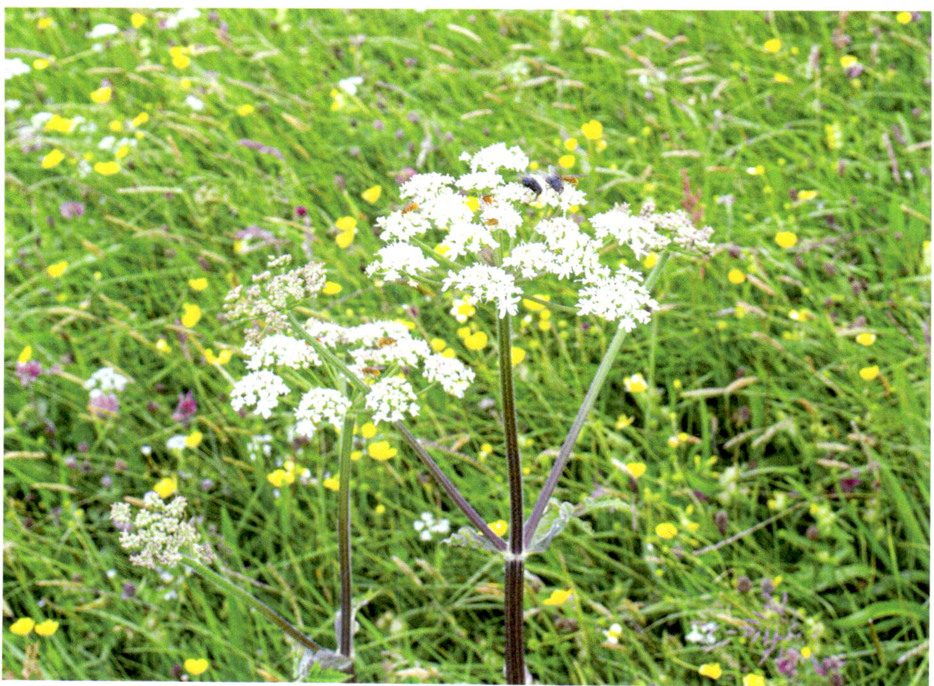

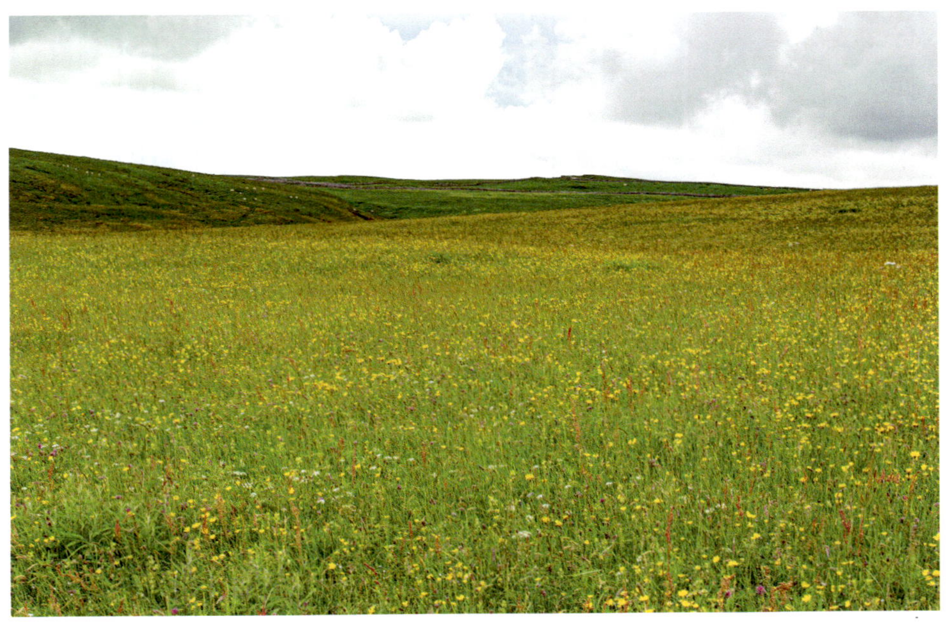

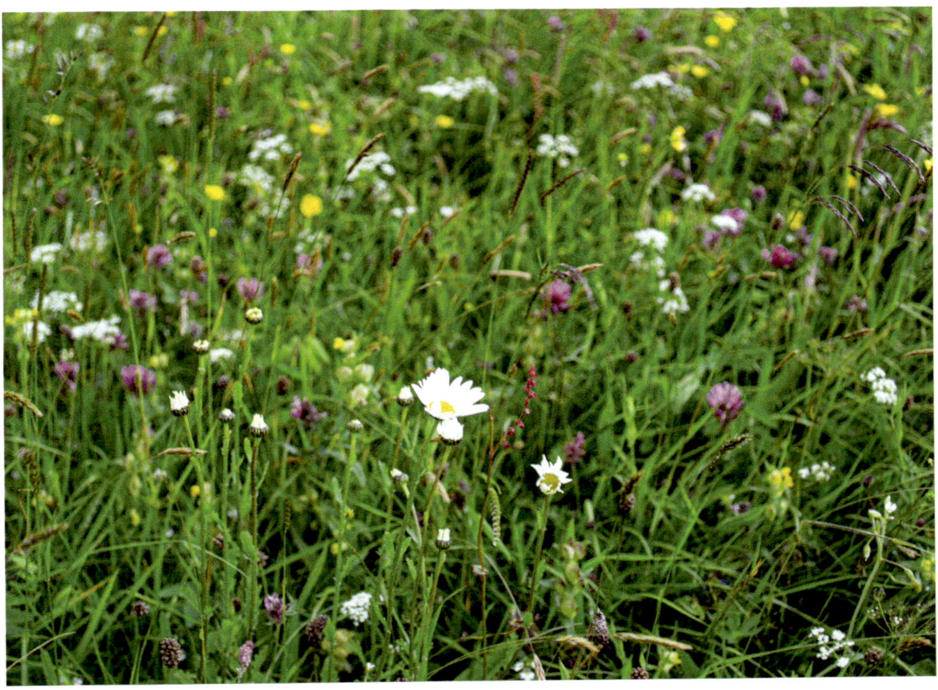

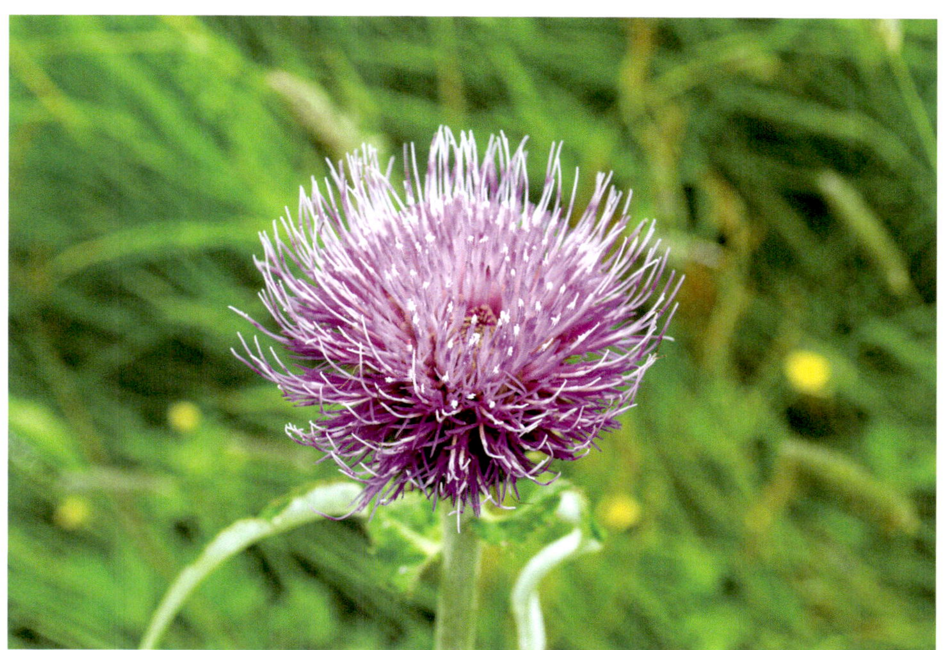

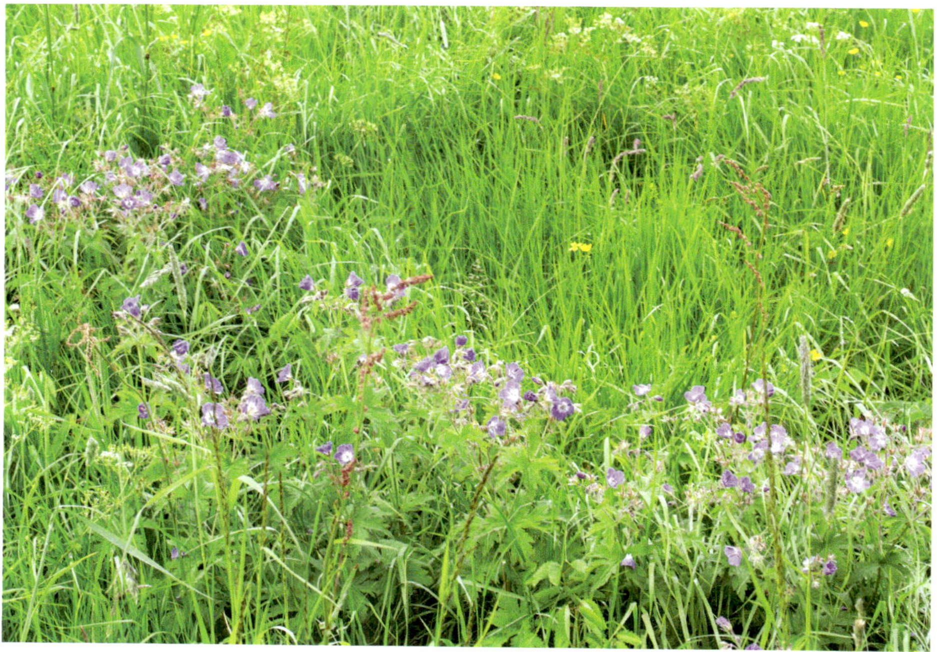

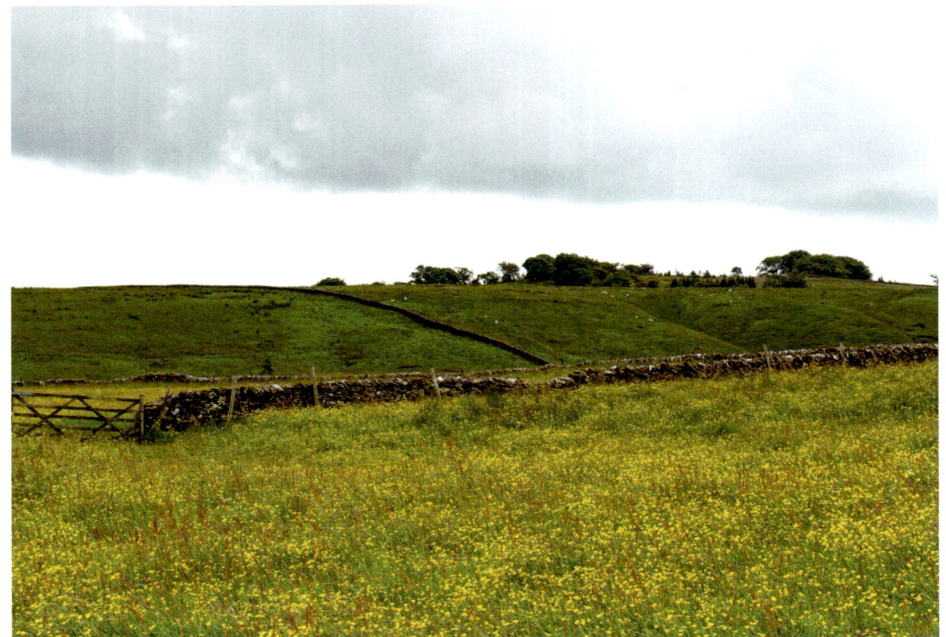

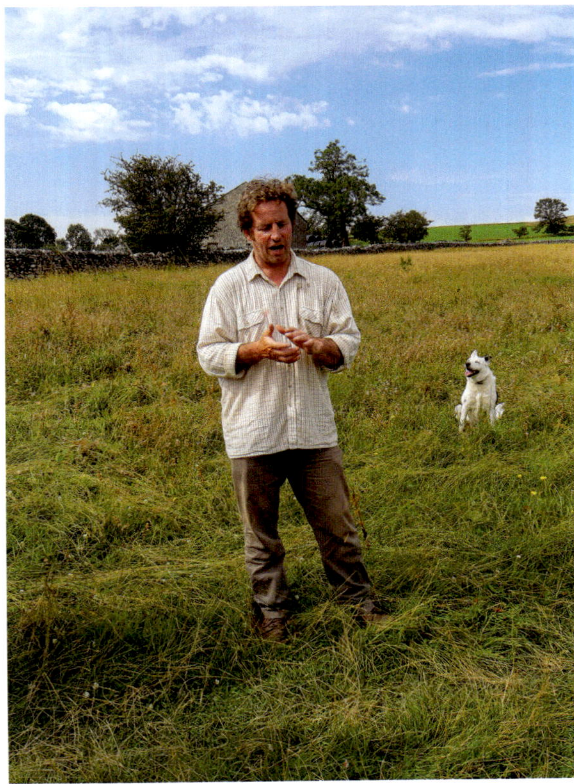

Neil Heseltine giving a talk to a group on his farm. (Judy Rogers)

Pubs

No trip to the Dales can be complete without a swift half after a long walk. Here are a few of my favourites.

Two for One!

We all do like a freebie! In East Witton, you can take advantage of a real two for one… 'Witton', as it was originally called, was mentioned as Witun in the Domesday Book. It means wood settlement, or where wood was worked. It was rebuilt by the Earl of Ailesbury, owner of Jervaulx, in the early nineteenth century with, remarkably, the houses and gardens replicated to the exact spots of an early seventeenth-century estate map!

Within the village are two great pubs: The Blue Lion and the Cover Bridge Inn. The former was a shooting lodge before being transferred to a coaching inn in 1840. Its name is taken from the Bruce family coat of arms which belonged to the Earl of Ailesbury, who once owned the local East Witton estate. The Blue Lion was run by the same family for three generations until Bessie Fletcher died in 1989. According to its owners, Bessie was well known in the area as she served beer in a jug straight from the barrel in the back and this was 'only available Monday to Saturday, that was if she liked the look of you. On Sundays, Bessie was the organist at the parish church and the pub was closed – no exceptions!' The next owners built the pub's first bar in the early 1990s, but renovations have been mindful of its Grade II listed status. It even has the original sign too.

The Cover Bridge Inn has been welcoming visitors since the sixteenth century. Previously known as the Foresters Arms and the Masons Arms, it is situated alongside the River Cover, a few hundred yards upstream from the confluence with the River Ure – and on the road from Jervaulx Abbey in East Witton to Middleham. Although the building is likely to be much older, the 'T' shaped part of the inn was built around 1670, when there was much development to cater for the drover's route up Coverdale twenty-five years later. Inside, it feels 'old' too, but in a nostalgic rather than tired way. There are open fires, wooden beams and a warm welcome.

The Tan Hill Inn

I've visited the Tan Hill Inn several times over the years and whilst the experience may differ depending on the season – and, in all honesty, the landlord – it never fails to fascinate me. The pub is famous across the globe. Its marketing strapline is 'the world famous'; not only because it is the highest pub in England at 1,732 feet (528 metres) but its folklore about punters being locked in for weeks when the snow descends.

What interests me is how the owners can scrape a living when the route out of Reeth can be snow-locked for weeks. Yes, it gets cleared and a hardy local or two – and curious tourist – will make their way up but that can't be enough to sustain income. Looking after the Tan Hill Inn has to be a lifestyle choice rather than an economic one! Anyway, it's easy to see why it's popular and it's not just the possibility of a lock-in. You can even get married there!

The pub dates back to the seventeenth century and was used as a hostelry for workers digging coal pits during the following century. The last mine at Tan Hill closed in 1929 but the pub had built up enough custom to keep on going – even after the miners' cottages around it were demolished.

As well as being a focal point for tourists, it is a beacon of safety too. Set on the Pennine Way, it's a welcome sight on the 268-mile journey from Edale to Kirk Yetholm. Plenty of people have camped around its grounds and once upon a time, you could also stay within the confines of the snow plough. Camping is welcome (there is a charge) and you can also book in for breakfast.

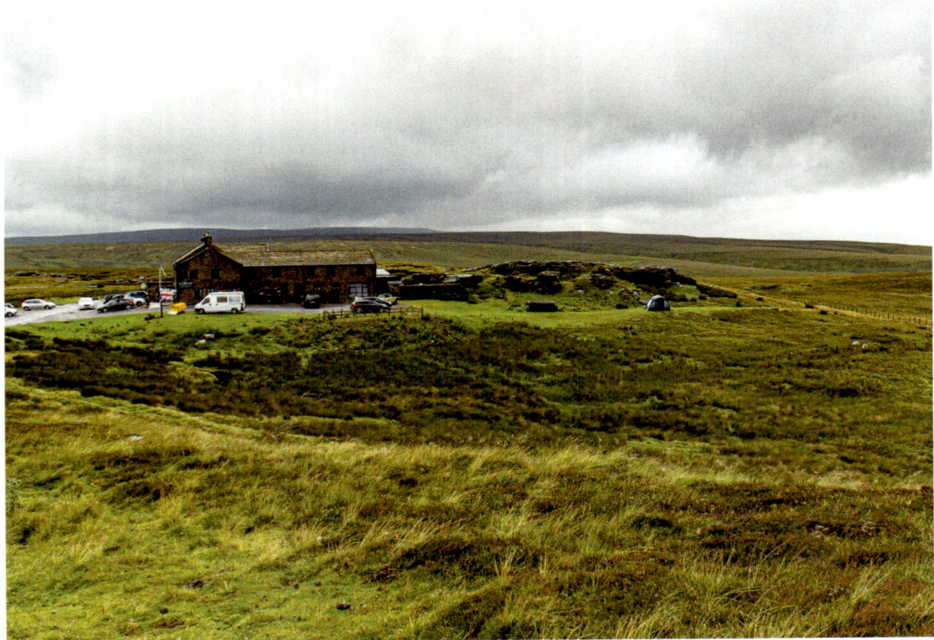

The highest pub in England.

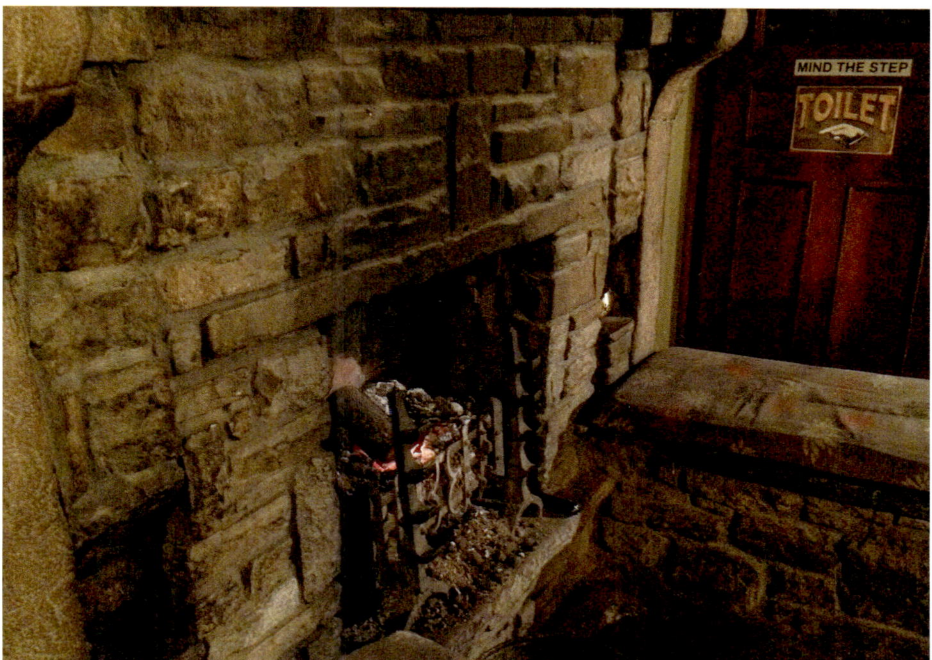

Tan Hill Inn's fire has, apparently, never gone out.

The Black Bull, Reeth

Classed as the unofficial capital of Swaledale, Reeth is a charming village in the north-east of the Dales, and not too far away from the aforementioned Tan Hill Inn. So, there's another two-for-one opportunity if you have a designated driver. It's where Arkengarthdale meets Swaledale which has been carved by the river bearing its name.

The village's oldest pub is the Black Bull which dates from 1680. You can't miss it because the sign above its front entrance is upside down in an apparent two-fingered salute to National Park officials. Previous landlord Bob Sykes attempted to tidy up the building by removing its render to not only expose the original 250-year-old walls but to also comply with English Tourist Board accommodation grading requirements. However, the National Park felt differently and threatened legal action if it wasn't replaced. They argued that it would have been rendered some years ago and therefore it should be in keeping with its original facade. Upset at this, a moody local turned the sign upside down in protest at the attitude of Park officials – and although it has moved from its original spot, it is still that way around!

The Black Bull has had some work done since my first visit but still retains its original character. Just up the road is The Buck, a coaching inn dating back to around 1760. It is at the point where a toll was charged to passing travellers.

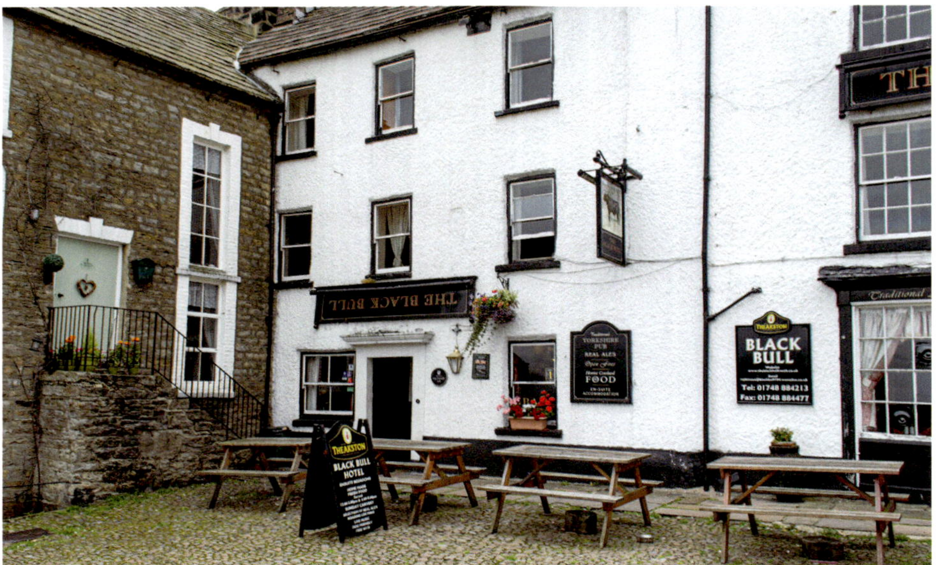

The Black Bull in Reeth.

The Fountaine Inn, Linton

In 1660, a young man from the village of Linton went to London to seek his fortune. He became a timber merchant and by luck would have it, held that occupation during two major events in the history of London which ironically meant that commodity would be in great demand: the plague of 1655 and the Great Fire the following year. Being named an Alderman soon followed and by the time of his death in 1721, he'd amassed a good fortune.

In his will, Richard Fountaine wanted to ensure his money would be put to good use whilst giving something back to the area where he grew up. He bequeathed a large sum for a charity to be established to benefit the local community in Linton. It had three facets; firstly, it had to be used for the benefit of the poor, and secondly, it necessitated the building of an almshouse – later called the Fountaine Hospital – to accommodate six poor men or women of the parish. Designed by Sir John Vanbrugh, the architect of Castle Howard, it cost £1,500.

Each beneficiary would have a small house within this hospital, with a chapel nearby which they needed to attend whenever prayers were being taken. Qualification was: 'They shall be poor persons who have been resident in the area of the Ancient Parish of Linton in Craven for two years preceding the time of appointment.' They would also have, yearly, a gown of blue cloth lined in green. Finally, the charity would provide a fund to pay for a rector, as long as they resided in the parish and said prayers twice a week.

Today, some of the requirements in Richard's will are still met. Six self-contained cottages are within the hospital and the trustees of the will – administered

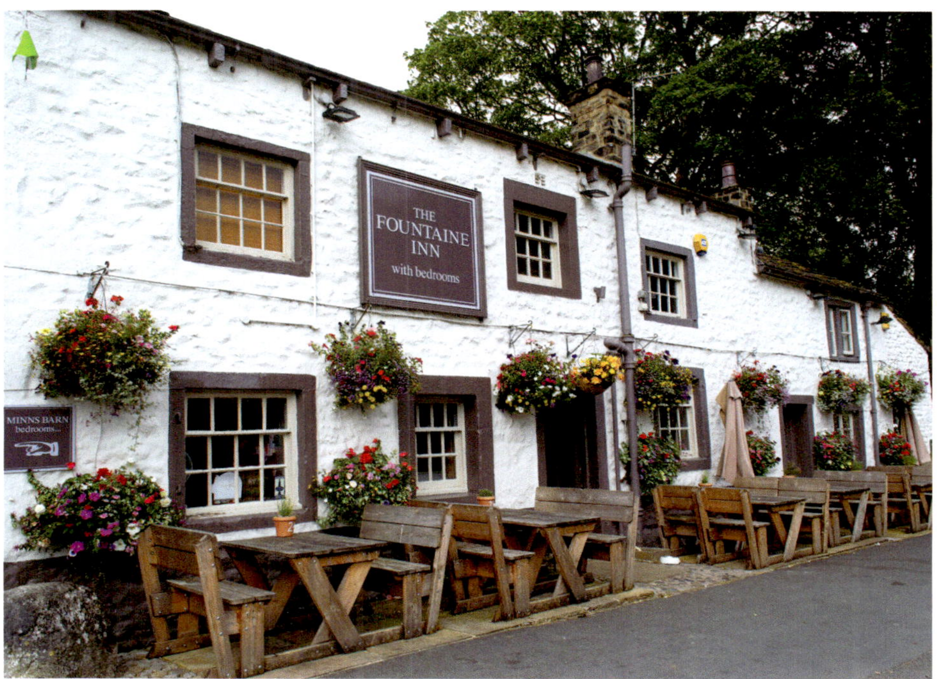

Linton's Fountaine Inn is beautiful ...

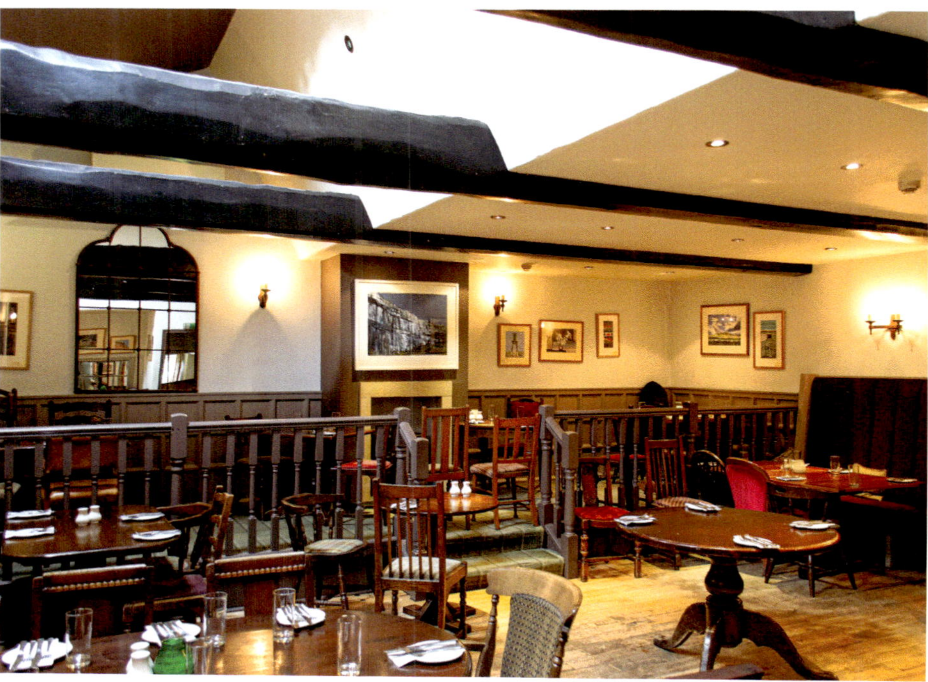

... and all keeping with the inn's and the village's heritage.

by twelve people from the ancient parish of Linton – have no difficulty in finding residents. The will also makes grants to students, apprentices and parish residents.

It seems only apt that the only pub in the village, The Fountaine Inn, is named after Richard. It is probably the most beautiful in the Dales if you're looking for something idyllic after a day's walking. With the pub at the back of you, the Fountaine Hospital is on your right. In front is the village green with brook and clapper bridge built in the late nineteenth century. The Fountaine Inn itself was likely built in the eighteenth century and is certainly snug inside. The bar area is on the left, with a larger room for dining up the stairs. It has a log fire, low ceilings and wooden beams.

The Game Cock Inn, Austwick

Another two for one! The Game Cock is home to one of the snuggest pubs in the south of the Park, but also a bakery which is a destination in itself early doors. It is a 'traditional with a French twist' place to eat but still a 'real' pub where you can pop in for a pint of Thwaites after a walk to Norber Erratics. The bar area has wooden flooring and seating around the walls to enhance its size, whilst there is also a wonderful elevated platform almost offering privacy away from the main area.

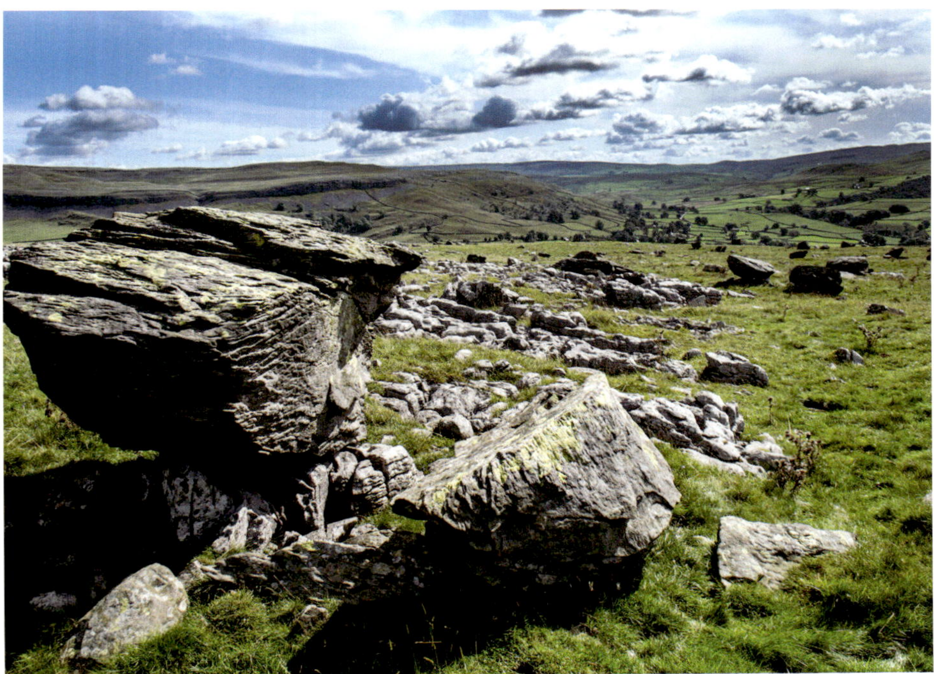

The Norber Erratics are just a short walk from the Game Cock in Austwick.

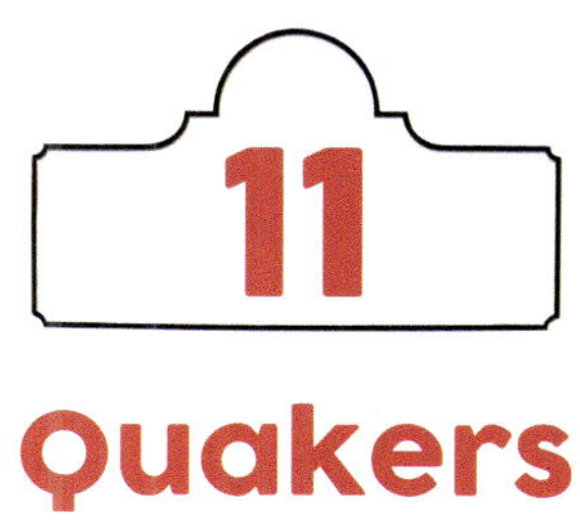

Quakers

I chose to pen a few words on religion to demonstrate how this special place draws people from all backgrounds together. The Dales has a strong Methodist tradition and is also considered to be the birthplace of the Quaker movement. George Fox, founder of the Religious Society of Friends, chose Firbank Fell in Sedbergh to address a crowd of more than 1,000 who had come to hear him preach. Nearby is Brigflatts, one of the famous Quaker meeting houses dating back to 1675. It welcomes more than 2,000 visitors each year and was built at a time when Quakers were suffering persecution and would have been fined for meeting. The Friends would congregate here but originally bought a small bit of land as a burial ground on the opposite side of the road because they wouldn't go to the parish priest to be buried.

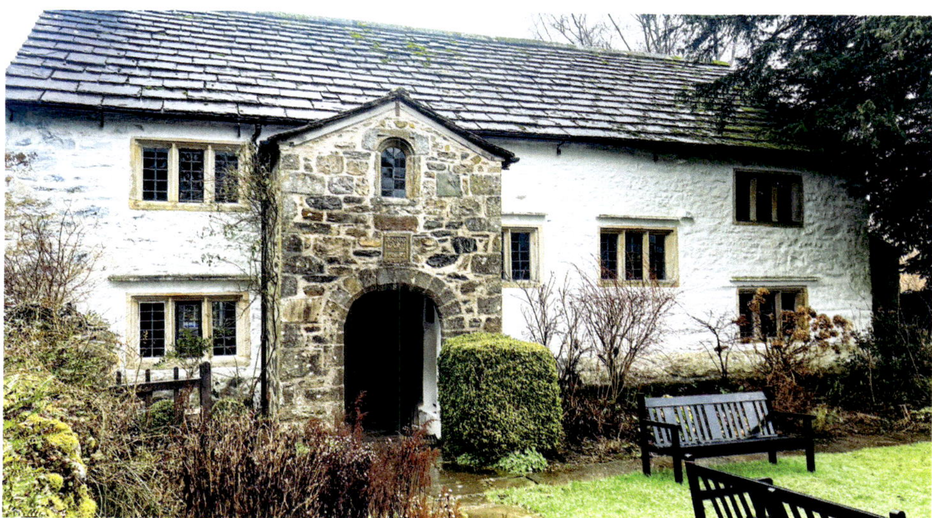

The Friends house in Brigflatts.

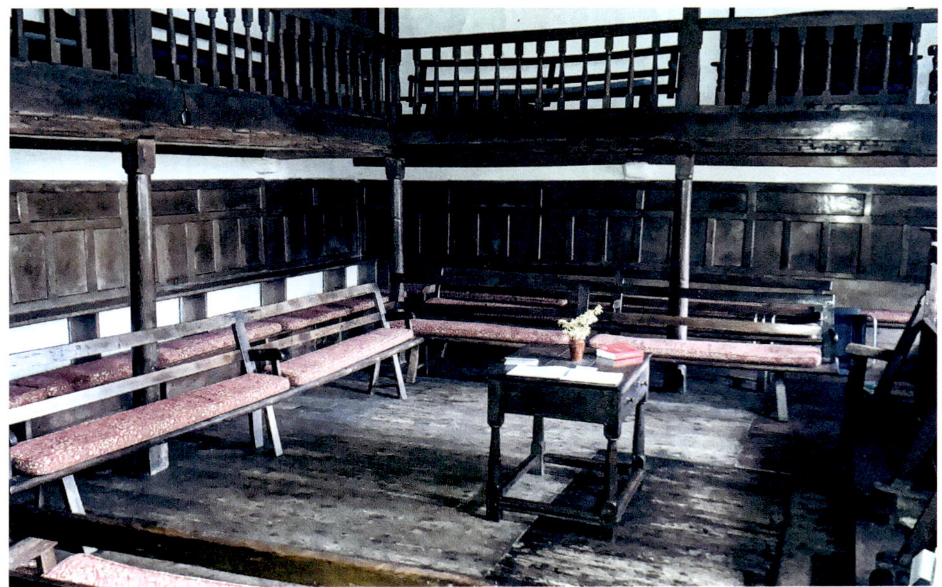

Above: Simple …

Below: … and peaceful inside.

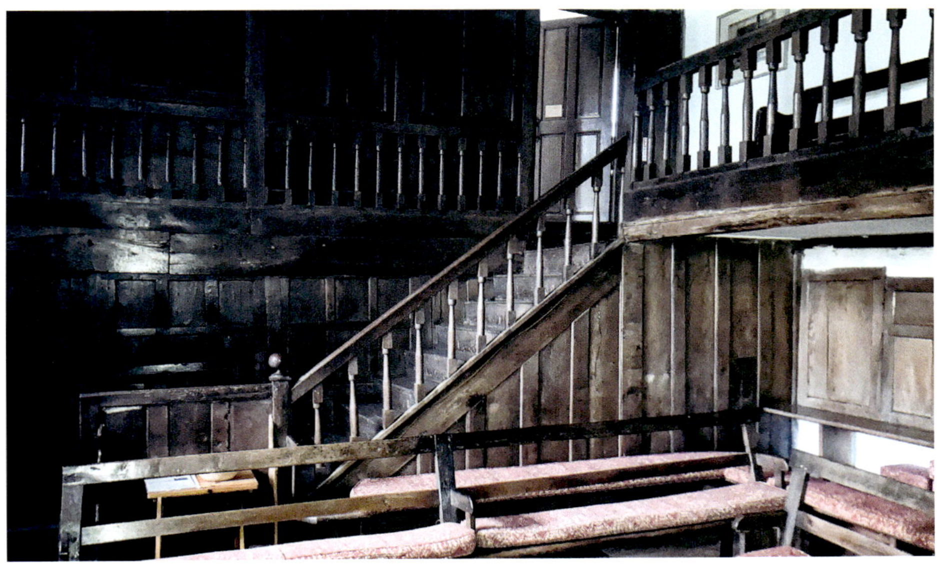

A plaque in the graveyard reads:

Rebecca Langle was the first Friend to die here and was buried in 1656 in, what was then, Richard Robinson's Apple Orchard. Four more Friends followed and then, in 1660, the land was bought from Richard Robinson for the sum of 10 shillings. This Burial Ground is then perhaps the first piece of land purchased by the early Religious Society of Friends. Since the 17th century some 700 Friends have been buried here although there are fewer than 100 identified plots. The raising of headstones was only sanctioned by Friends nationally in 1850 (the earlier dates on some headstones may reflect memorials being raised to Friends who had died in earlier years). In keeping with the Quaker Equality Testimony, headstones are of a uniform size and shape.

Angus Winchester, Professor Emeritus of Local & Landscape History at Lancaster University, told the *Countrystride* podcast – www.countrystride.co.uk – that Fox believed Christ came to teach his people that there is something within us we can reach into that will act as a spiritual guide. 'Quakerism is very much a personal religion in that sense,' Angus said. 'If we gather and focus on that seed, we can find the answer to life's questions and how to live a good life.'

Fox was born in Fenny Drayton in Leicestershire in 1624 and was a troubled young man looking for truth in religion. He would visit various religious teachers but could never find what he was looking for. He sought purity in life, and in developing his own words said people could forget about all the structures of formal religion.

Being a dissenter, George's life was somewhat spent either in trouble or trying to avoid it. He was imprisoned several times for blasphemy – even being threatened with execution at one point – and for causing a disturbance.

'Fox wasn't the only preacher travelling around at that time, and there were lots of people who were looking for religious truth,' Angus continued. 'He travelled from Leicestershire up into Yorkshire and spent a fair bit of time in the area. He has people who have, as he would say, been convinced of the truth of what he's saying. He climbed up a high hill, which we now know as Pendle Hill, and saw some sort of vision of people waiting to be gathered. He then travels to Garsdale and into Sedbergh.'

It's clear that when Fox spoke people listened and he was mixing in circles that featured plenty of dissenters and alternative views. He had an entourage he would travel with, and that would give him more gravitas when he arrived in a place. At Sedbergh, he chose the day of a fair to preach to what would be a captive audience, under a tree by the churchyard. A few days later, on 13 June 1652, he travelled to Firbank Fell because that was where a meeting of separatists known as seekers was being held. To a crowd of more than 1,000, he spoke for nearly three hours.

The site, now known as Fox's pulpit, features a small plaque which says let your lives speak – a fundamental aspect of Quakerism. It's an unremarkable site but an obvious place of pilgrimage and solace.

Quirks and Traditions

The Dales isn't alone in having its peculiar way of doing things. Whilst researching this book, I found several traditions, and dare I say it, little quirks that should be celebrated.

I'm not sure if this is just a Yorkshire thing but when someone gets married in Askrigg, local children will tie the churchgates together with baler twine. It's up to the best man, change in hand, to pay off the mischievous kids before he is allowed to cut the gates free.

At the opposite end of the life celebration spectrum, when someone is buried, a funeral cake will be made. They link back to the Arval bread of the Vikings and are shortcake-like biscuits, decorated and flavoured with caraway seeds. Usually, they would be wrapped in paper printed with the deceased's favourite verse or hymn. The cakes are given to visitors to the household and those attending the funeral. At the Dales Countryside Museum, you can see a hand-carved wooden stamp that was used to decorate the cakes in the late nineteenth century.

Another foodie tradition is cheesecakes. Janet Rawlins wrote in *A Dales Countryside Cookbook* (1993) that they were 'traditionally made in Swaledale on the Fridays before Whitsuntide and Midsummer festivities, and eaten with the joint of beef instead of the usual bread'. They featured at Muker's 'Aud Roy' communal celebrations that would begin with a group of local lads wearing large aprons. They held these out to collect offerings from women, who threw cheesecakes, Yule cakes and cooked meats.

In Wensleydale, the Redmire Cheesecake Gatherers had baskets and wore fancy dress when collecting for Redmire Feast – a tradition which continued up to 1910. The cakes were made with cheese curds, rather than cream cheese, mixed with other ingredients to make the filling. Sadly, the tradition no longer takes place, but they still hold a domino drive.

Time for a more sinister tradition … the Burning of Old Bartle takes place at West Witton on the first Saturday and Sunday after St Bartholomew's Day. In the evening, after a day of fell running and other festivities, an effigy known as 'Old Bartle' is taken through the village before it is burnt. During the wander, and as far away from the traditional country gala as you can get, an ancient verse is chanted, depicting the chance of 'old Bartle' which some speculate could be St Bartholomew or a sheep rustler.

> At Penhill crags he tore his rags, At Hunter's thorn he blew his horn, At Capplebank Stee he broke his knee, At Grassgill Beck, he broke his neck, At Waddam's End he couldn't fend, At Grassgill End we'll make his end, Shout lads shout!

Grim…

In Bainbridge, the blowing of the forest horn would take place at 9 p.m. between 28 September and Shrove Tuesday. *A Dictionary of English Folklore* (2003) says that 'some have tried to link it (the hornblowing) with Roman times, but it is more likely to date from when Bainbridge was the administrative centre of the Forest of Wensleydale, and the sound of the horn was designed to guide benighted travellers to safety. This would date it to medieval times, but the first known mention is in 1823.'

If you're near Malham, then it is worth seeing the strange triple stocks (just for the sake of it really) and the watery grave at the church of St Michael the Archangel at Kirkby Malham. The history of the internment stems from Colonel John Harrison's career in the army. His wife Helen asked that 'as water parted us in life, so it shall in death', and so her grave was built over a stream running through the graveyard. The plan was that John would be buried on the other side of the stream but sadly the gravedigger couldn't get through the hard bedrock to create a separate grave, and they were buried together.

Thanks to Susan Briggs at Dales Discoveries – www.dalesdiscoveries.com – I found the preceptory of the Knights Templar between Swinithwaite and Aysgarth on the A684. Here, you can see the remains of a small chapel, an altar and three stone coffins. According to Historic England:

> A preceptory is a monastery of the military orders of Knights Templars and Knights Hospitallers (also known as the Knights of St John of Jerusalem). Preceptories were founded to raise revenues to fund the 12th and 13th century crusades to Jerusalem. In the 15th century, the Hospitallers directed their revenue toward defending Rhodes from the Turks. In addition, the preceptories of the Templars functioned as recruiting and training barracks for the knights whilst those of the Hospitallers provided hospices which offered hospitality to pilgrims and travellers and distributed alms to the poor. From available documentary sources it can be estimated that the Templars held 57 preceptories in England. At least 14 of these were later taken over by the Hospitallers, who held 76 sites.

A preceptory at this site is first mentioned during the period 1170 to 1181 when timber for buildings was granted by Roger de Mowbray from his Forest of

Nidderdale. It was originally centred on land 150 metres to the north of Temple Farm before moving half a kilometre up the hill to the south. The original site was abandoned by 1202 with the current preceptory occupied until 1307.

Historic England also says the 'pre-Templar field system survives as a series of banks forming regular fields in what is known as a coaxial field system. The banks of the field system are extensive and can be traced across much of Wensleydale. Parts of the system are visible across the monument. Examples survive in the field between Long Bank Wood and the road, where at least three banks survive, and the field just south of Wellclose Plantation where at least five banks survive.'

Finally, and in no way connected with Templars, we turn our ears to music. At Christmas, carols would regularly be changed to fit a more local slant. The Yorkshire version of 'While Shepherds Watched' was often sung to the tune of 'Ilkla Moor Baht 'At' whilst the 'Wensleydale Carol' is still sung regularly in the Dales.

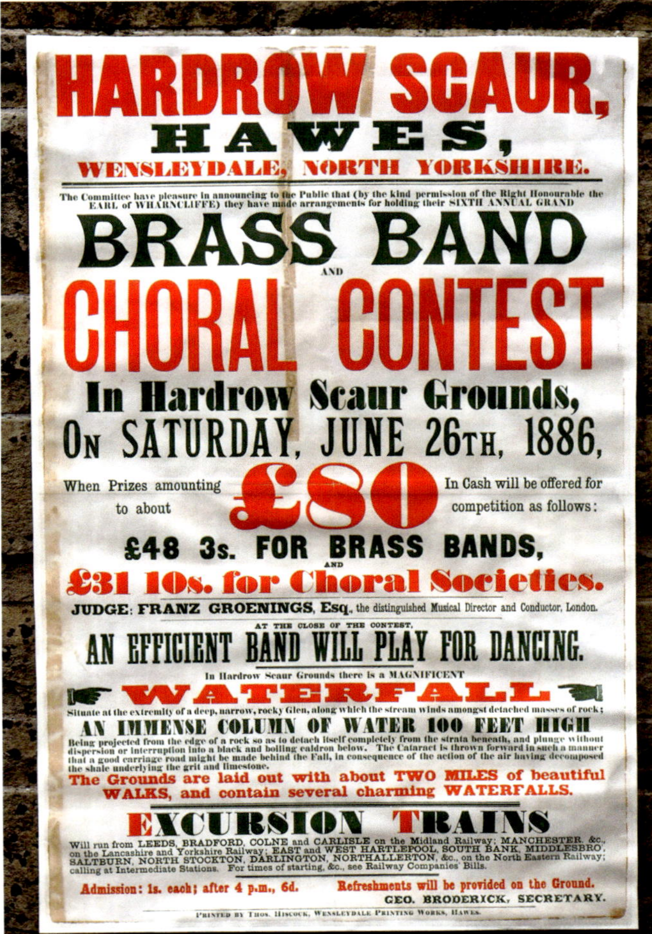

Hardrow Scaur (Hardraw Force) is the perfect venue for a brass band. The acoustics are amazing because of the shape of the landscape. This poster for the event on 26 June 1886 was printed by T. Hiscock of Wensleydale Press in 1886. (Dales Countryside Museum, Yorkshire Dales National Park Authority)

There is also a strong revival of traditional Dales music through the Dales Music and Dance Collective. They are a small group of singers and instrument players from across the Dales who come together to revise monthly music sessions in the Buck at Buckden in Upper Wharfedale and across the Park. The resurgence of this cultural heritage of music was down to the late Bob Ellis who wrote *There'll be none of that lazy dancing*. He researched the tradition of Dales' dances and music and presented a fine collection of folk tunes and dances from the Yorkshire Dales.

Bob was a keen melodeon player and Morris dancer as well as being Head of History at the Wensleydale School. He joined the Swaledale Mountain Rescue team, enjoyed caving and rock climbing, managed Askrigg Football Club and had a keen eye on local history.

Mark Sheridan from the Dales Traditional Music and Dance Collective gave the eulogy at Bob's funeral. Part of it read:

Bob had begun to play for Crook Morris on returning north. Soon he was travelling to festivals and sessions and gaining his reputation for teaching beginners and improvers and leading sessions. The steady pace sessions at Whitby and Sidmouth with their associated tunebook; the visits to Witney and the establishment of Melodeons in Wensleydale; the 'Loose Knit Band'; his involvement with French music through Les Pannards and his visits to explore cajun music; and then perhaps his greatest legacy: his research into, and revival of, the music and dance of his beloved Dales. In 2023, Bob was awarded a well-deserved Folklore Society award for his achievements. I must apologise for only scratching the surface here ... there is so much more. He even has his own keyboard layout for the melodeon named after him! Above all Bob brought people together. He made things happen. Bob may no longer be physically with us, but I am sure his legacy will live on in so many different ways.

And so it does. You can find the Dales Music and Dance Collective at: www. dales-music-and-dance-collective.org.uk

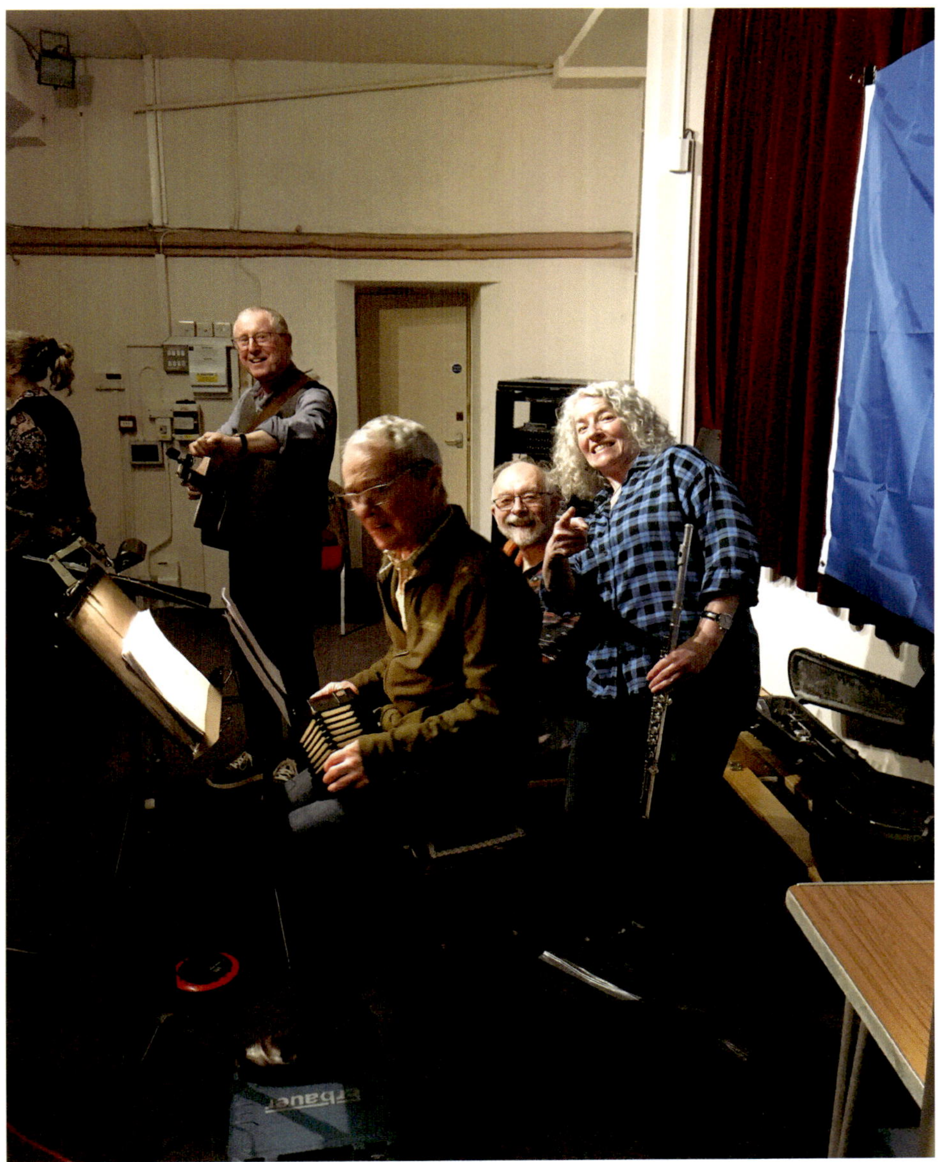

The late Bob Ellis – a legend of the Dales' music scene. (Mark Wallace)

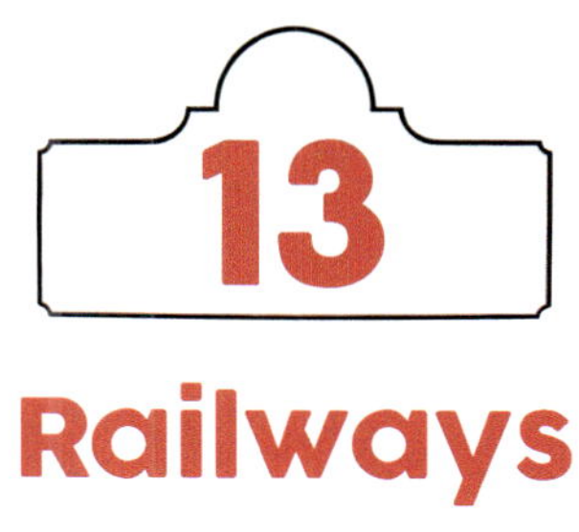

13
Railways

Ribblehead Viaduct's twenty-four arches support the weight of the Settle-Carlisle Railway, one of the most magical ways to reach the three peaks. Trains slow down to cross the structure that overlooks vast areas of moor and the home of the navvy camps that built it. The line's roots stretch back to the 1860s when the East and West Coast Main Lines linked England and Scotland. The Midland Railway struggled to negotiate terms with their operating rivals if they wanted to move freight or people beyond their boundaries. To relieve the pressure, they looked at building an alternative route from Settle to Carlisle to avoid lengthy, protracted discussions. After agreeing on a line, the company was successful in gaining Parliament's permission, but no sooner was that granted than relations with rival rail companies improved. Midland asked for the decision to be reversed, but that was rejected.

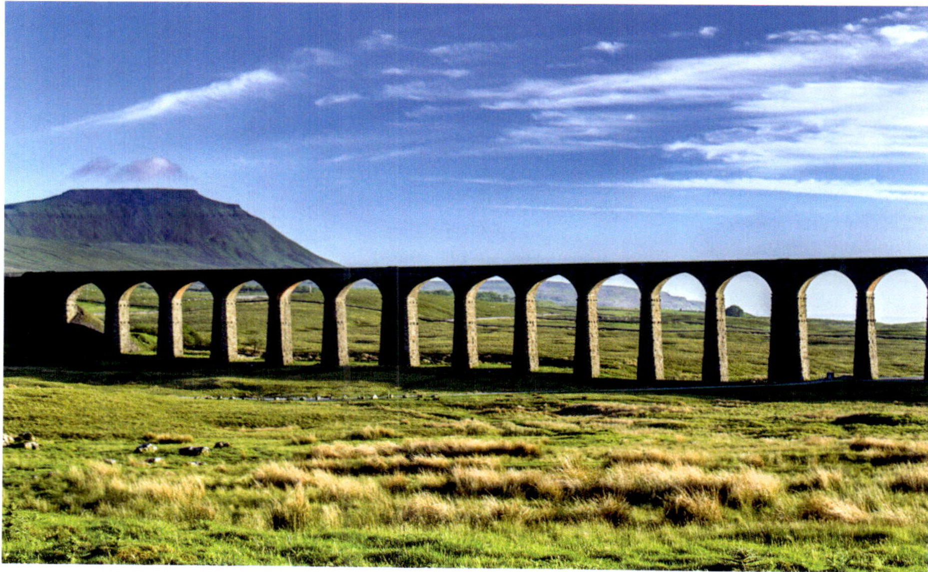

The iconic Ribblehead Viaduct.

Construction began in 1869 and was completed in seven years, with around 6,000 men working across the 73-mile route. The line was opened to passengers on 1 May 1876, with freight having been carried for the first time roughly a year previously. In 1968, the service became entirely diesel-operated, but most local stations – apart from Settle and Appleby – closed in 1970. Eleven years later, recommendations were made to close the route to passengers, mainly because of the sheer cost of weatherproofing the viaduct. A project manager was even appointed by British Rail to close the line, but instead, he encouraged passengers to use it. However, such was its success that local stations reopened in 1986. Three years later, the government backed his approach and services still operate.

Amazing as the line is, Dr David Johnson says we aren't giving the viaduct its real name. Writing in his *Discovery Walks in the Yorkshire Dales* series:

> The correct name for the viaduct is Batty Moss, not Ribblehead Viaduct. Why Batty, you might think? Now this is a true story! Mrs Batty ran a popular shebeen and, by all accounts, was a very forceful and domineering lady. As might be expected Mr Batty was mild, inoffensive … and henpecked. In the end he conceived a dastardly plan! He persuaded the wife to tie him up and push him into a deep pool. She obliged with the first part but was thwarted on the second. In the nick of time he jumped aside and his dearly beloved fell headlong into the pool and drowned. Could there be a moral here? Originally the station here was to be called Batty Wife station … but perhaps Ribblehead sounds better.

Sadly, there was no such Mr Batty-style reprieve for the Wensleydale line that once connected to the Settle-Carlisle. It remained as a single-track branch line transporting milk and stone from Northallerton to Garsdale, but the passenger service closed in April 1954. One passenger train ran each way between Garsdale and Hawes until March 1959, and in April 1964, the line between Redmire and Hawes closed completely. Now, the Wensleydale Railway operates heritage diesel train services between Scruton and Leyburn, and the hope is enough money could be raised to reopen the station at Redmire.

Hawes station is now the location of the Dales Countryside Museum which has an interesting exhibition on railways, among many others, and a stunning railway carriage outside.

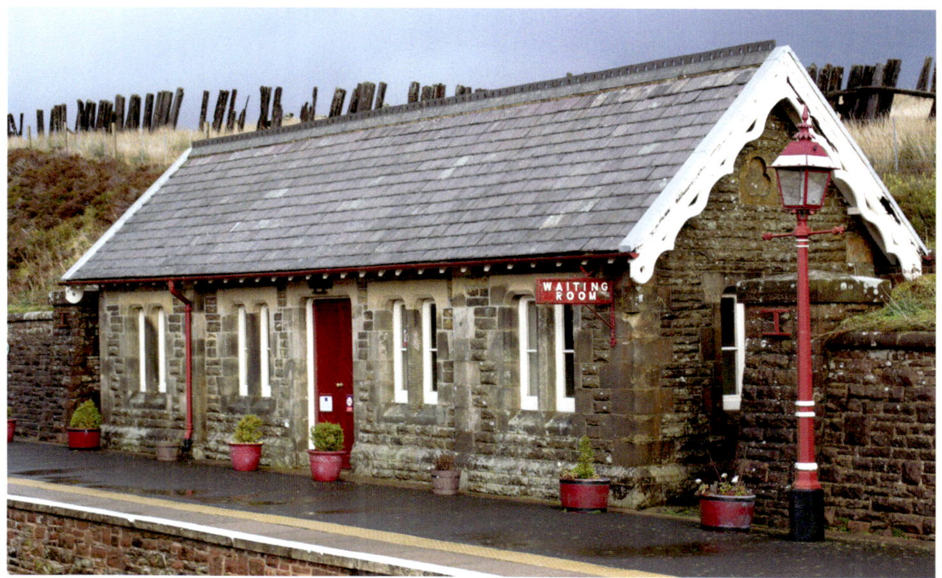

Above: Dent station – one of the most remote stations in the country.

Below: Dent Head Viaduct.

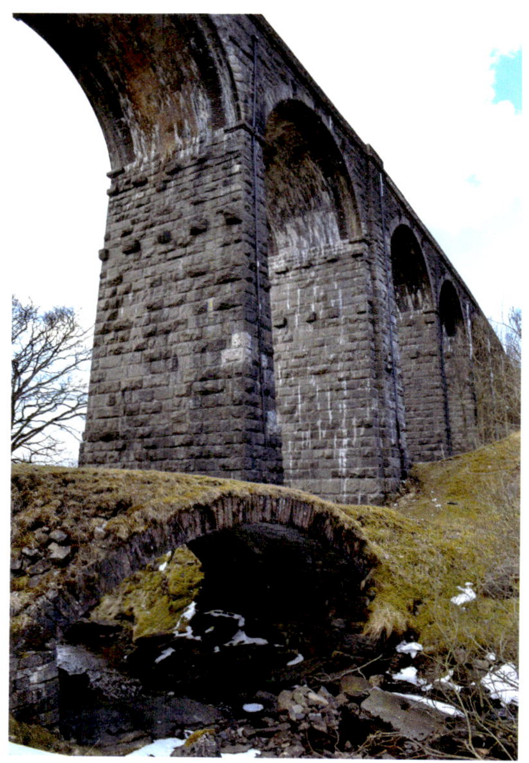

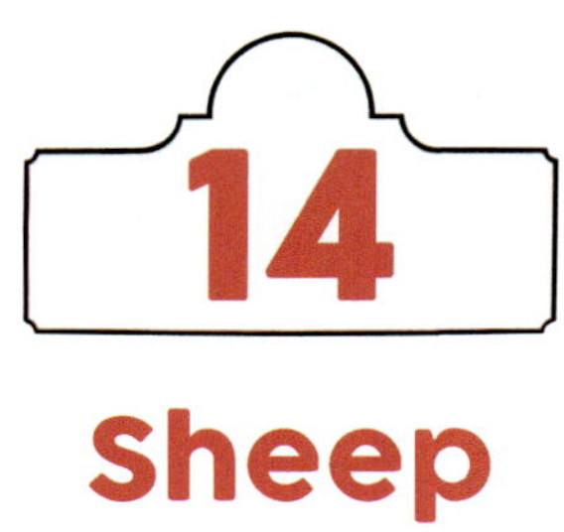

Sheep

There may be sheep of all different types across the Dales, but there are only a few that genuinely come from the area. One breed, the Dalesbred, is indigenous to the fells as it can cope with the harsh environment and good pasture grazing. Sadly, it is a breed at risk and is therefore on the native breeds register, which helps to raise its profile and protect the work of generations of farmers.

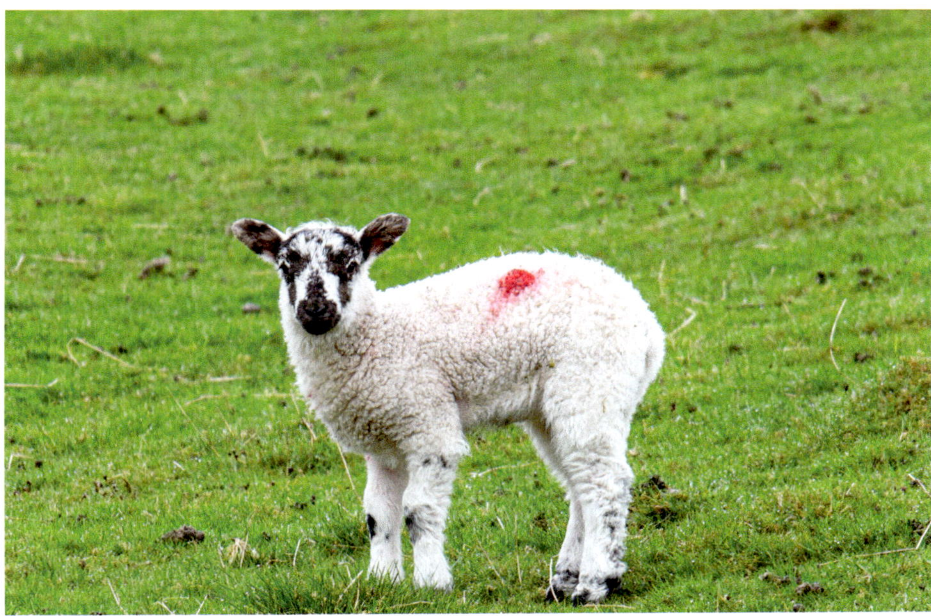

A familiar sight in the Dales! A lowly sheep (not a Dalesbred!).

John Dawson farms at Bleak Bank near Clapham and is Chair of the Dalesbred Sheep Breeders Association. In 1925, the Swaledale and the Dalesbred Sheep Breeders' Association split to become two separate associations. Some members wanted to breed sheep with different specifications that matched what they and the market wanted, but both associations agreed that the sheep's ability to withstand the harsh weather conditions and to breed and rear their lambs on the high Dales hills had to remain the same. The first annual meeting of the Dalesbred Sheep Breeders' Association was not until 1946, and it has been well-attended ever since.

John champions the breed alongside the value of British farming and British wool. He's part of a project that sends wool to Glencroft in Clapham, where they make stunning and premium knitted jumpers. In return, he receives a fair price for the wool, much higher than the standard, which sees farmers losing money.

'It is fantastic what Edward at Glencroft is doing,' he said. 'Using our wool and others around the area helps the Dalesbred breed and also shows the value of the product. It's not just about the financial aspect of the wool, though, it's what it is compared to other non-natural products. We're not going into the North Sea to get it or down a coal mine to bring it up. It has so many properties that are useful, from clothes to house insulation. It doesn't pollute waterways because it's a living thing. It's a growing thing and so undervalued. It's a shame that we don't use wool as much anymore or natural fibres. Here, wool grows on Ingleborough and is used locally. Yes, it costs more, but you don't need to replace it for a long time. What's not to like?'

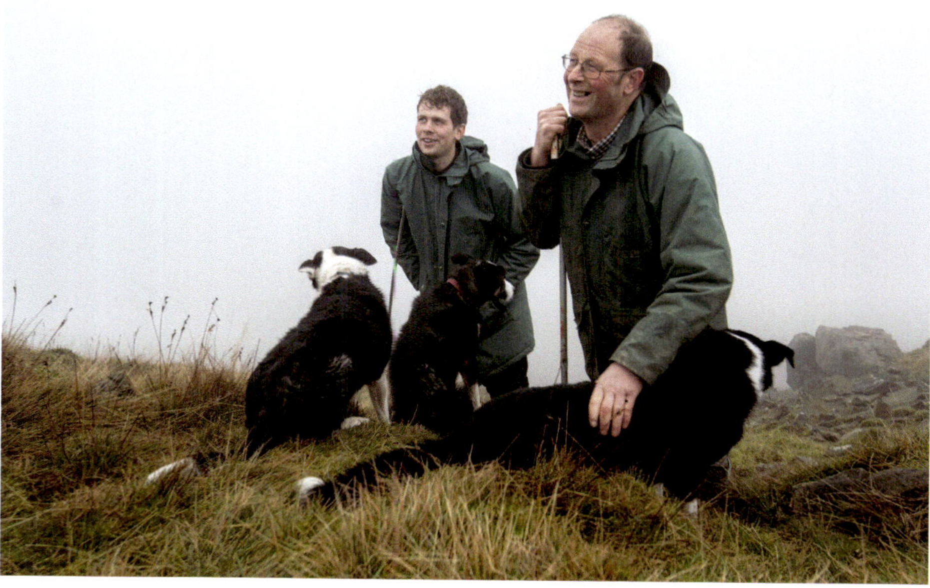

William and John Dawson at a misty Ingleborough summit for the start of the gathering. (Rob Fraser/somewhere-nowhere)

John's family arrived at Bleak Bank as tenants in around 1920 but didn't bring any sheep with them because they were already hefted on Ingleborough. The sheep came with the tenancy; they belonged to the farm and that stock effectively helped to pay the rent.

'I've always found that quite fascinating,' John said. 'I think it is because you don't own the sheep, yet in a way you do. We can trace the roots of this breed back to the enclosure movement. The sheep know which part of Ingleborough to graze on because they have been taught by their mothers. That lineage has been handed down over the generations and is part of this area's cultural heritage. Bleak Bank's flock has effectively been on this land for generations.'

John is a fourth-generation farmer at Bleak Bank with his wife, Judith, and son Will. Five times a year they will head up Ingleborough to gather in the sheep, joining eleven other farmers who work on the mountain. It's a time to check how their flocks are doing but also to catch up with old friends and keep a traditional way of working on the common going. Once these traditions are lost, they are very hard to resurrect.

Half of Bleak Bank's sheep are bred for replacement stock and the other half are crossed with Teeswater's to breed the maximum size of lamb.

'The hefting thing is terrific, that's how the sheep live,' John added. 'When we are gathering, you can see the sheep peeling away from each other because they know where they need to go. It is really enjoyable working with your neighbours, your dogs, and farmers who want to farm. The first gathering is in June for

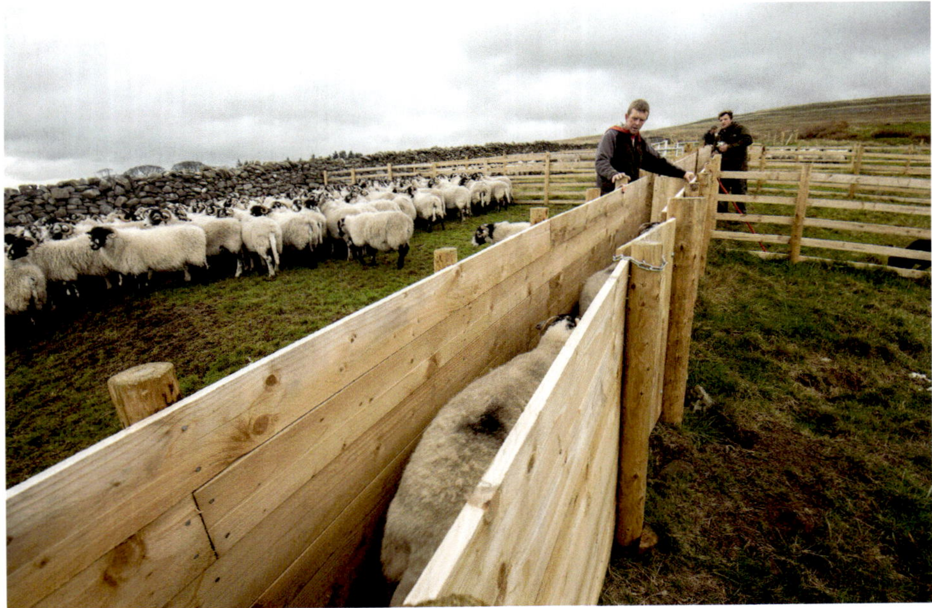

Ingleborough graziers sorting ewes in new pens at Cod Bank during the gathering. (Rob Fraser/somewhere-nowhere)

shearing; we gather twice in August, once for dipping and then spaining at the end of August, which is when we take the lambs off the sheep, and the mothers go back to the hills without them. We then gather again in October to prepare them for tupping time. Ingleborough is closed at the end of October for grazing through winter because it helps the fell recover and is part of the government scheme we are in.'

John farms cattle as well as sheep at the farm and is involved in local initiatives such as curlew conservation. He believes farming isn't valued in terms of what it produces to feed the world but also the impact many land managers have in delivering real biodiversity benefits to the land. It's a rewarding job.

'I cannot believe not everybody wants to be a farmer. I have no wish to do anything else,' John said. 'I walk down our yard, and I see sheds that my dad built. I feel very privileged that I get to look at the view every morning. I'm getting the cows in when it's coming light in the morning, and even if I am a bit late, I still try and spend just a couple of minutes looking right down around the valley just to see what's what.

'My great-grandmother's son was killed in the war and there was no grave. She would walk up the fields here and look at the railway station down to Clapham because she always hoped that he may find his way home. I often think of that when I'm stood up in the fields because she would be looking at that very same view.'

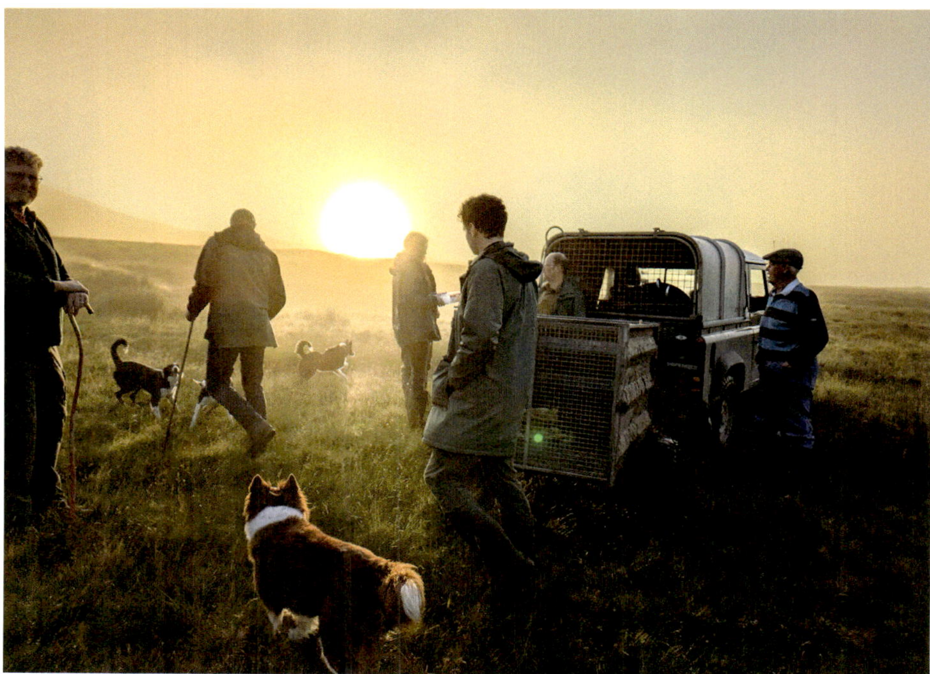

Up at the crack of dawn! A late summer start for the gathering. (Adrian Shepherd)

Sports and Games

In such a varying environment, it's no surprise that fell running has been popular in the Dales for many years. Village shows usually feature running events, whilst the Three Peaks Race over Pen-y-Ghent, Whernside and Ingleborough takes place annually from Horton-in-Ribblesdale. It is one of the pinnacles of sporting endeavours, with the current course a challenging 23-mile navigation, despite the route being paved in several places to protect the mountains.

Originally starting from Chapel-le-Dale, the first race in 1954 had just six starters and three finishers. Fred Bagley, of Preston Harriers, won in an impressive time of three hours and forty-eight minutes. Andy Peace of Bingley Harriers ran the course record of two hours forty-six minutes and three seconds in 1996, whilst the women's record is held by Victoria Wilkinson of the same club with three hours nine minutes and nineteen seconds in 2017. Both these marks were set over the new course from Horton-in-Ribblesdale.

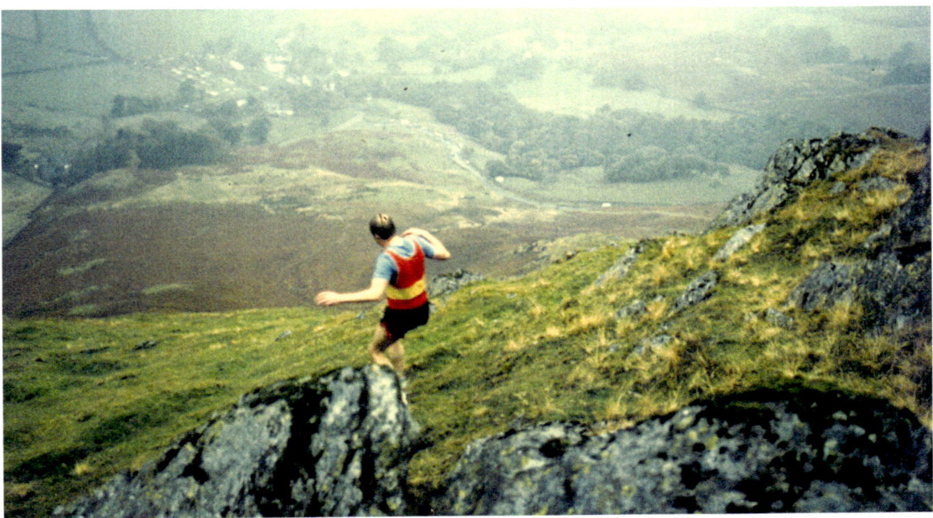

Fell runner and super coach Roger Ingham MBE running at the Embsay Fell Race in 1977. (Roger Ingham)

Fell running in the three peaks and beyond is captured in Victoria Benn's wonderful *Peak Performance*, and I would be doing the sport a disservice by condensing it into just a few hundred words. Her dad is Roger Ingham MBE, a real 'sports billy' of a man – international coach, athlete and font of all knowledge when it comes to many sports, including running, football, rugby union, rugby league, swimming and boxing.

Incidentally, the fell race isn't the only challenge on these famous peaks. The Three Peaks Cyclo-Cross entered its 61st iteration in 2025. Starting at Helwith Bridge, it is billed as the 'toughest and biggest Cyclo-Cross event in the UK'. Riders will race for 38 miles, around 17 of those on the road, more than 20 'off' and four or so when they have to carry their bike. It adds up to around 5,000 feet of climbing.

It's always been the case that working people would look for some kind of entertainment in their spare time. In the past, some of it was pretty brutal. The National Park's excellent Out of Oblivion website – www.outofoblivion.org.uk – mentions that the site of a possible eighteenth-century cockpit has been found in Stirton. It says: 'Pairs of cockerels were pitted against each other within the cockpit and they would often fight to the death. Rivalry between villages reached a peak at such contests. Cockfighting spurs have been found on the site in recent years. These steel spikes were attached using leather straps to the legs of the fighting birds to increase the viciousness of the attack. To the west of the village lies Cock Hill.' The Upper Wharfedale Museum in Grassington has an original cockfighting trophy along with a pair of those iron spurs. Bull baiting was another 'pastime' with Askrigg, Grassington and Ingleton still having large iron rings set into the ground in their marketplaces. Such pursuits were thankfully banned in the nineteenth century, and that meant people had to find much more appetising pleasures which reflected modern standards.

Quoits is played from April to September. It involves the throwing of metal, rope, or rubber rings over a set distance, to land over, or near, a spike. You can see the 'surfaces' or grids for this game in many places including West Burton where they are sat right in the centre of the village green. Knur and Spell is a long-gone sport but should make a comeback for me! There's an example of the contraption used in the game at the Dales Countryside Museum. The spell traps the knur, and when the trigger is touched with a pommel or stick it throws it into the air. The idea is that the player swipes at the projectile and tries to thrash it as far as they can! At the museum, it says that the biggest 'knock on record with a pot knur is above fifteen score yards; a wooden knur has been sent over eighteen score yards'. That's around 275 metres with the pot and close to 330 with the wooden.

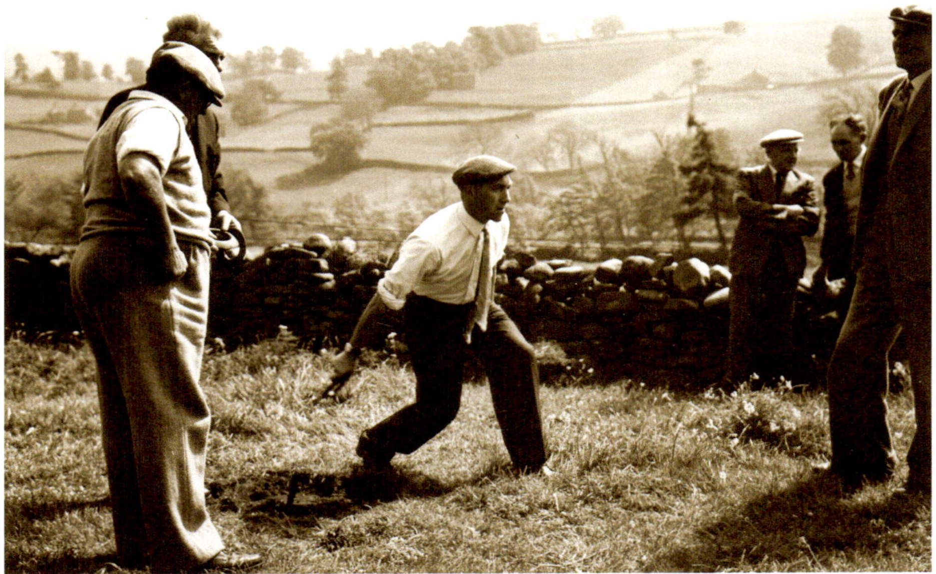

A group of men playing quoits at Rowleth Bottom Sports in Swaledale in 1965. The player is throwing the quoit as he stands beside the hob or marker, whilst a judge is watching the thrower's feet to make sure that he does not overstep the mark! (Dales Countryside Museum, Yorkshire Dales National Park Authority; courtesy of the Estate of Marie Hartley)

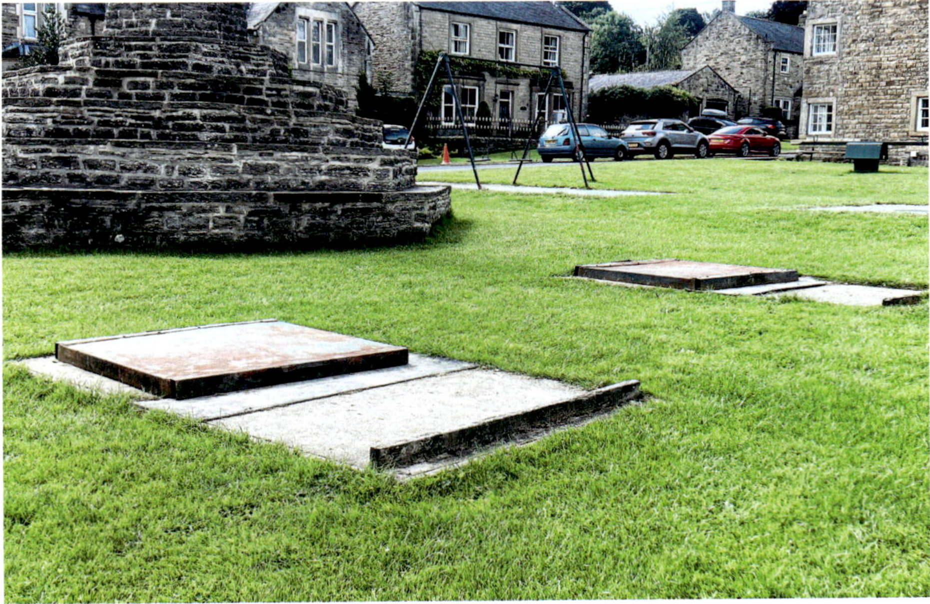

Quoits are still played today across the Dales – these are quoit pits in West Burton.

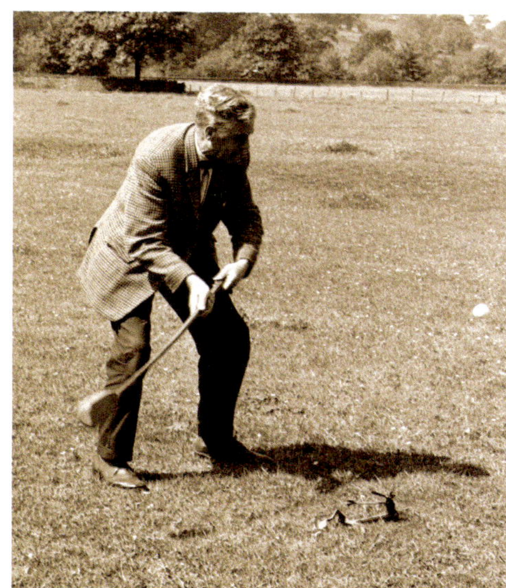

Mr Tom Peacock of Reeth is about to give the knurr a good hiding! (Dales Countryside Museum, Yorkshire Dales National Park Authority; courtesy of the Estate of Marie Hartley)

Wallops is a bit like skittles and is a prominent feature at several events, including the Redmire Feast. Sticks are thrown at nine pins, a contest fiercely contested but was only played by men and women. Perhaps stick-throwing was too dangerous for kids back in the day?

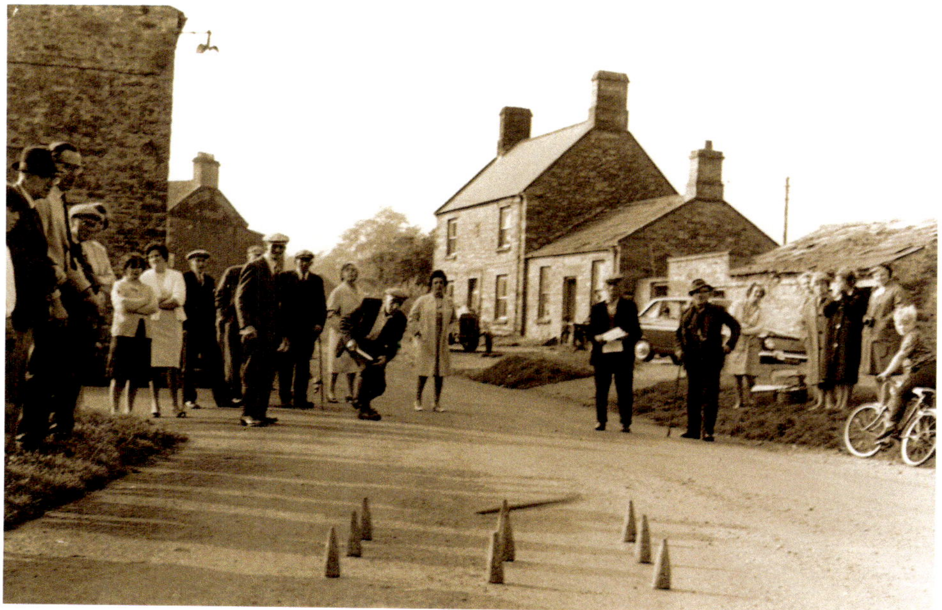

Wallops being played on the road at Redmire Feast on 26 September 1966. You can see the player aiming to hit the nine conical pieces of wood. (Dales Countryside Museum, Yorkshire Dales National Park Authority; courtesy of the Estate of Marie Hartley)

Village Fetes and Shows

The village fair is the staple of country life, a chance for people to meet, sample food and strong beverages, and win competitions. In the Dales, they were mostly historically 'trade' shows when thousands of cattle would be sold. They grew around droving tracks and routes across the fells and in villages such as Leyburn and Kilnsey. 'Best in show' for these animals duly followed, as did all the sports and traditional games, standing the test of time for all to enjoy until the pandemic enforced a halt. Some were lost – Malham used to host a dinosaur trail which may come as a surprise – but thanks to committed volunteers, several are still taking place.

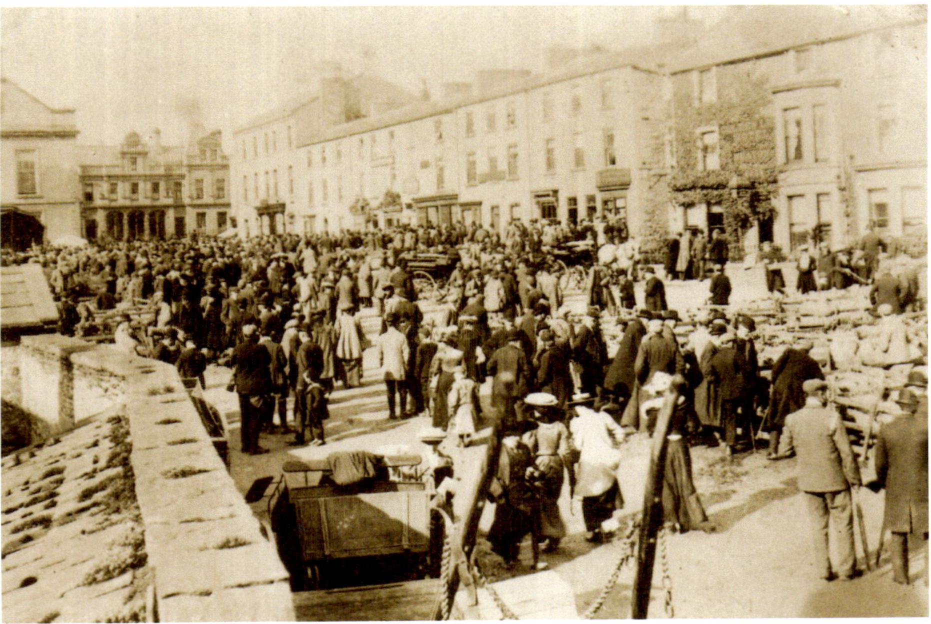

The sheep fair at Leyburn, taken in October 1906. Pens of sheep are huddled downslope from the Golden Lion Hotel and others are in front of the Town Hall. The view is taken from a wall top at the back of the Shambles, looking up the marketplace toward the Town Hall. (Dales Countryside Museum, Yorkshire Dales National Park Authority)

The Cuckoo Festival in Austwick, held every May, celebrates the story of the spring visitor who likes to occupy other bird's nests. Winters in the Dales can be particularly harsh, so any sign of spring and better weather ahead is a source of joy to embattled residents who have had to layer up in the colder times. The cuckoo is seen as a sign that those warmer times are coming – and a tale says that the people of Austwick were so pleased to see one nesting in a tree that they built a wall around it in the hope of keeping it there. They believed if the bird stayed in the village, they would keep the balmy temperatures all year round. Sadly, the wall they constructed wasn't high enough and it simply flew away.

Up the road in Ingleton is a 1940s festival which celebrates 'old-time' nostalgia. The village is turned over to the atmosphere and poignant history of wartime. There are living exhibitions, military vehicles travelling through the streets, amazing food, and you can watch ''40s fashionistas strut their stuff on the catwalk and visit our hairstylist to recreate the glamorous looks of the era'. Their words, not mine.

Malham Show is a real tourist attraction and has all manner of events including sheepdog demonstrations, Punch and Judy, fell faces, drystone walling

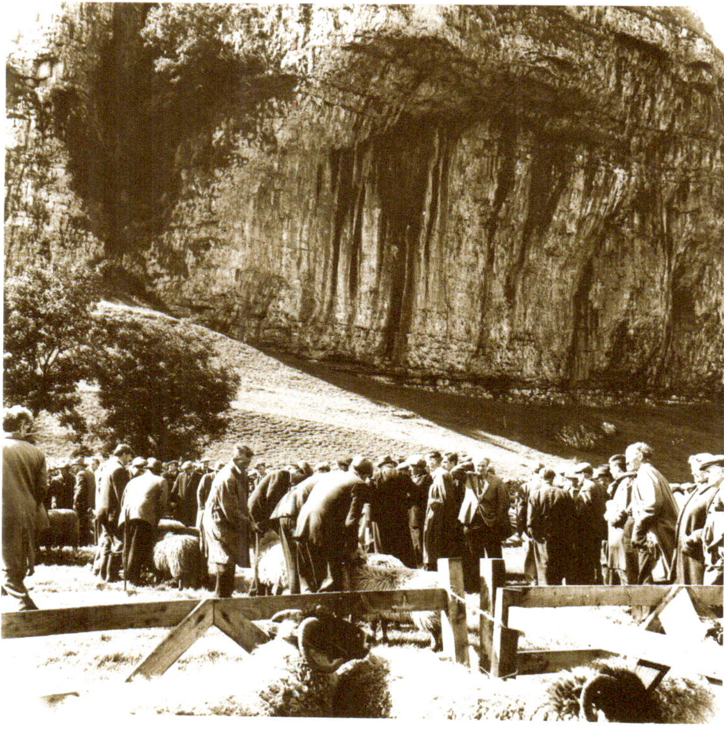

Sheep pens at Kilnsey Show with a line of sheep being judged, in the shadow of the impressive Kilnsey Crag. (Dales Countryside Museum, Yorkshire Dales National Park Authority; courtesy of the Estate of Marie Hartley)

competitions and a lot more. It is held every August. Kilnsey Show has been running since 1897 and is held on the Tuesday after the August Bank Holiday. Its remit is to promote and showcase farming in the Yorkshire Dales, and it features the famous crag race where runners tackle the western side of Kilnsey Crag. It's an impressive sight watching athletes of all ages and abilities take on the almost vertical challenge! The show is packed with livestock competitions, equine events and sheepdog trials, together with baking, handicrafts, horticulture, speed sheep shearing, birds of prey, and Longton Sheepdogs.

The Castle Bolton-Redmire feast is as grandiose as it sounds with lots of traditional sporting competitions such as wallops and quoits, and a huge 'bring and share tea' which encourages people to eat and talk together. In 2024, if your surname began with A to N, you were asked to bring sandwiches or savouries and N to Z, something sweet. Superb!

The May Day celebrations in Long Preston see local schoolchildren dance around the Maypole in the village, just outside the inspirationally named Maypole pub. The *Craven Herald* says it is thought to be one of only seven left in the country where children are invited to perform the traditional maypole dance to celebrate the arrival of summer in a ceremony that dates back to medieval times.

The community plays a real part in the Settle Flowerpot Festival too, which runs annually over the summer. More than 150 installations appear around the streets of the town with an estimated several thousand flowerpots used to create

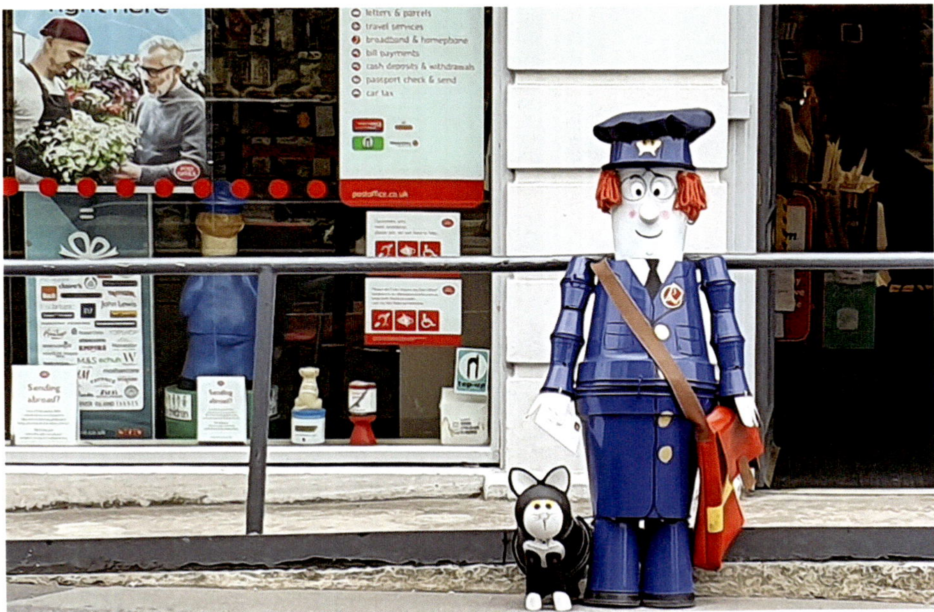

Above and overleaf: Some of the colourful exhibits from Settle's popular Flowerpot Festival. (Settle Flowerpot Festival)

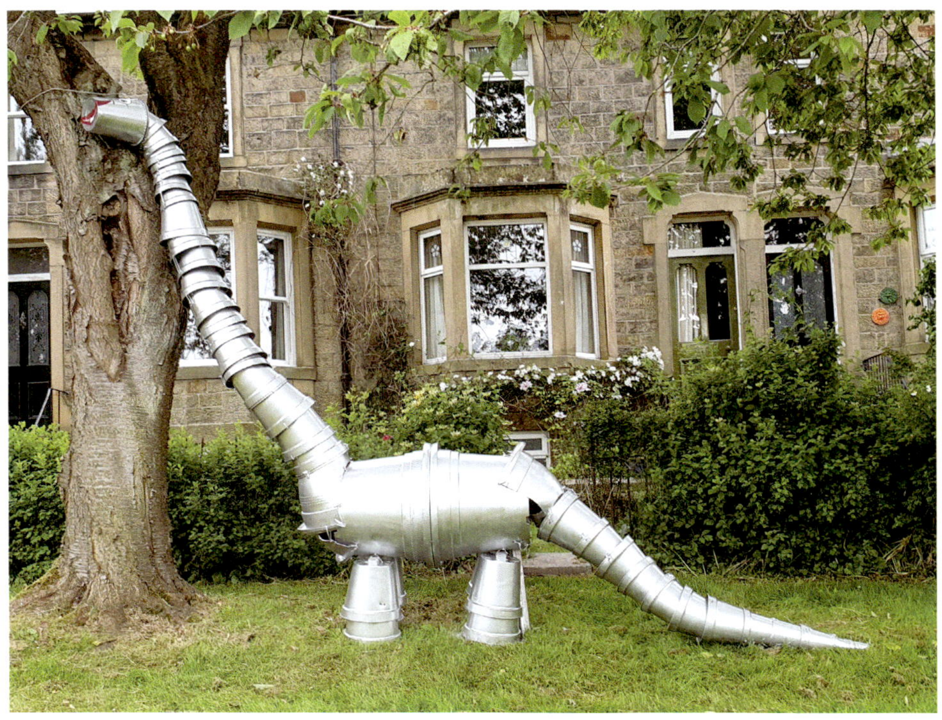

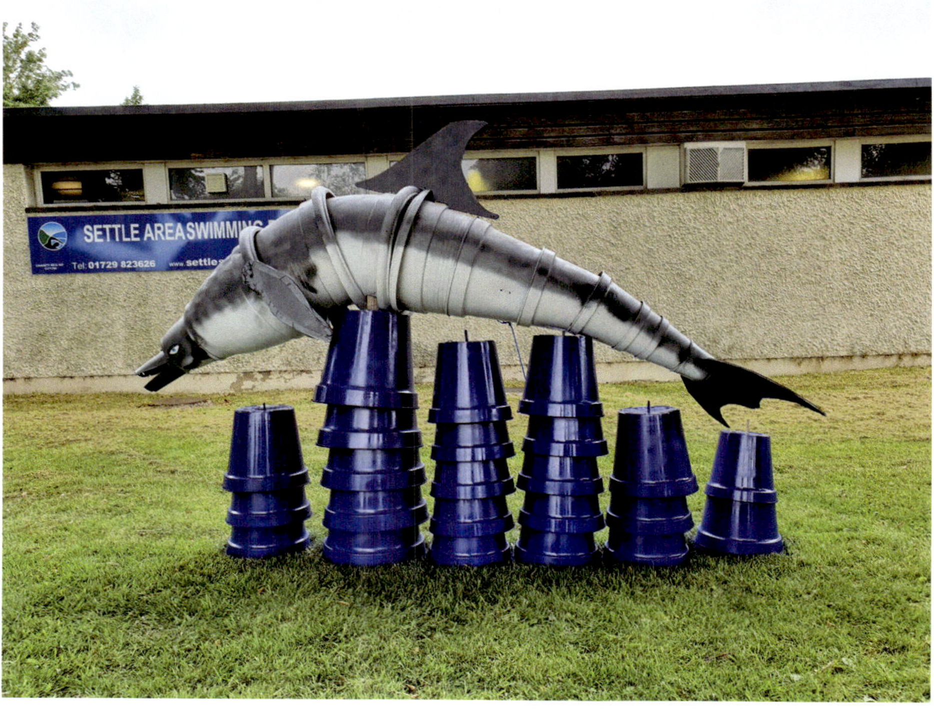
SETTLE AREA SWIMMING
Tel: 01729 823626   www.settle

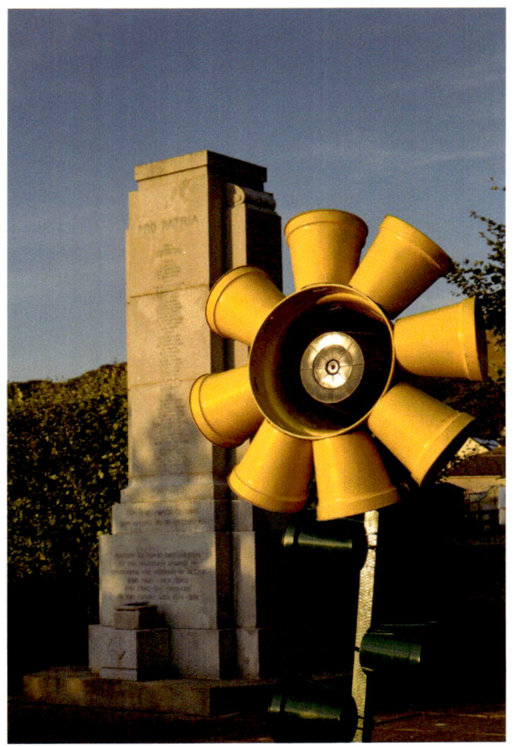

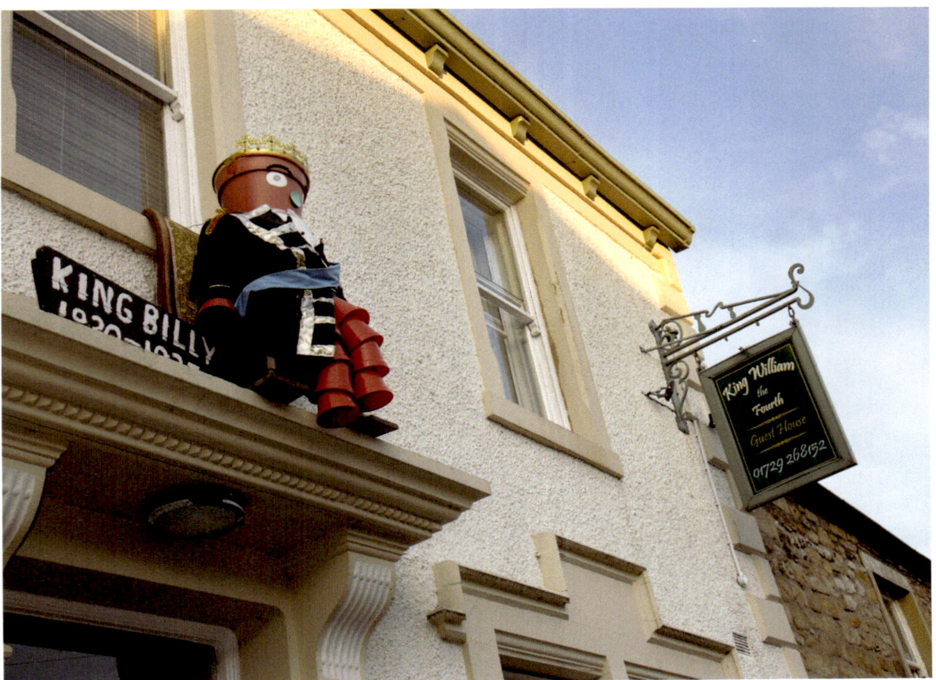

KING BILLY
King William
the
Fourth
Guest House
01729 268152

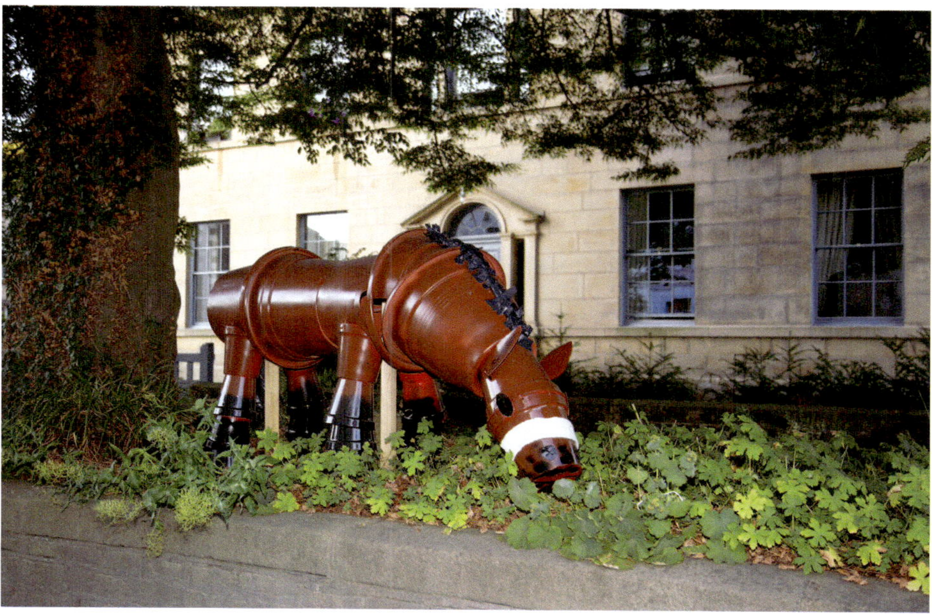

the diverse and entertaining exhibits. The organisers say that it attracts as many as 15,000 visitors over the July to September months. Remarkable!

Incidentally, just over the Park's border in Wigglesworth, they have the Wiggy Worm Festival, with flowerpots and other items creating colourful worms all over the village.